AND YET THE MELODY LINGERS

Essays, Sermons and Prayers On Religion and Race Volume 1

C. Anthony Hunt

AND YET THE MELODY LINGERS
Essays, Sermons and Prayers
On Religion and Race Volume 1

by C. Anthony Hunt
The Rhodes-Fulbright Library series

ISBN: 1-55605-385-1

Library of Congress Control Number: 2006926388

WYNDHAM HALL PRESS
Lima, Ohio 45806
www.wyndhamhallpress.com

Printed in The United States of America

4   C. Anthony Hunt

Table of Contents

INTRODUCTION and ACKNOWLEDGEMENTS

To speak of America is to speak of the ongoing convergence of religion and race. These are two themes that have continued to be intricately and indelibly linked – *and yet the melody lingers*. These twenty-two (22) essays, sermons and prayers offer snapshots of one person's thought and praxis with regard to the themes of religion and race in America.

Written over the course of a decade (1995-2004), the pieces that comprise this volume are a part of an ongoing journey - a litany of reflection/action - on these important themes. These writings can also be seen as a prayer that racism – and all of its atrocious effects - will someday be eradicated.

It has been my task as a teacher, pastor and program executive to offer constructive approaches to how we might move toward this end. I am thankful to God for all of the persons with whom I've had the opportunity of journeying thus far. I offer particular words of gratitude to Drs. Cecil Gray, Ira Zepp, Calvin Morris and Michael Gorman for their kind encouragement and urging on this and other projects. To my colleagues at the Multi-Ethnic Center for Ministry, where I served in ministry for over six years, I am profoundly appreciative of how – together – we sought to model God's call that we become an inclusive church. To Bishops Felton Edwin May, Marcus Matthews, Alfred Johnson, Hae Jong Kim, John Schol, and Jeremiah Park, I am eternally grateful to each of you and consider you mentors and friends on the journey. Thanks to each of you for your prophetic leadership of the church.

To colleagues in the academy – at St. Mary's Seminary and University, Wesley Theological Seminary, the Graduate Theological Foundation/Oxford University, and the Center of Theological Inquiry at Princeton University – I offer thanks to you for offering contexts for the thoughts herein to be "fleshed out" through learning, reflection and teaching.

To my parents Amelia, William and Shirley, thank you for being great parents. To my siblings, grandparents and extended family thanks to each of you for modeling what it means for us to be family.

And to my wife Lisa, and our children Kristen and Brian, I continue to marvel at your generosity in allowing me the explore ways that God calls me to be the best that I am to become.

To our late son Marcus William Hunt – who passed from this life on August 7, 2005 – you embodied the words of Christ – "Blessed are the pure in heart, for they will see God." It is to your life and ongoing witness that I dedicate this volume.

Finally, I offer thanks and praise to God in Christ, who is my Reason. May God continue to bless each of us in the days ahead as we strive to become the church and society that God calls us to be.

SECTION ONE
-Chapter 1 -

O LORD, OUR LORD
(A PRAYER FOR THE CHURCH)

(This prayer was offered at the Baltimore-Washington Annual Conference of the United Methodist Church in June 1999 in Washington, DC.)

O Lord, our Lord,
How excellent is your name in all the earth.
You have created us a little less than the angels.

How excellent is your name, O Lord,
In our diversity and yet in the oneness – the unity
that is offered in thee.

O Lord, our Lord,
How excellent is the beauty of your holiness,
The beauty of the wonderful tapestry
that is your multi-colored, multi-cultured,
multi-dimensioned people.

How good and excellent it is
that we come together with the various deep streams
that is our faith – from north to south…east to west –
joined together in Christ who makes us a new creation.

Joined together in our physical presence today,
Your daughters and sons who are God's creation
of many nations and tongues.

From home to home…
and from neighborhood to neighborhood…
and from nation to nation
we are joined together now to give you thanks and praise.

O Lord, our Lord,
 How excellent is your name.

Bless us, O God, that we would be mindful
 of your vision for your church and your world.

Bless us that we would realize – anew –
 those things that are required of us –
 that we would do justice, and love kindness,
 and walk humbly with you.

Bless us, O God,
 that we would heed your Great Commandment to love you,
 and to love one another as you have first loved us.

Pour out your Holy Spirit on us gathered here
 that we would learn to love unconditionally as you loved us
 in your Son, Jesus the Christ.

Bless us, O God,
 that we would learn to honor one another
 through our listening, and through our yearning
 to understand that which is beyond our comfort zone.

God, we humbly beseech thee now to bestow upon us
 A new hope… A more fervent faithfulness
 A more holy boldness…A more relevant and peaceful witness.

That our hearts would be rekindled by your spirit anew.
 And that we would be prepared
 for the kingdom that is to come in and through thee.

Bless us in the name of the One, Jesus,
 who came and suffered, and bled and died
 that we might have the right to eternal life.

In Jesus' name we pray. Amen.

-Chapter 2 -

CROSSING BOUNDARIES: REFLECTIONS ON OUR HISTORY, HERITAGE AND HOPE

(On March 31, 1998, the author was installed as the fourth executive director of the Multi-Ethnic Center for Ministry of the United Methodist Church in an investiture service at Asbury UMC in Washington, DC. This is his inaugural address for that occasion.)

First, let me say that I am honored to be here today. I want to give honor to Christ who is my Lord and Savior. I honor my family, which is my foundation – Lisa, my wife, and best friend and confidant... our three wonderful children – Marcus, Kristen and Brian who are the wonder of life, and make every moment, of every day worth cherishing.

To my parents, William and Amelia Hunt, who have paved the way through their nurture, example and faith – words cannot express my gratitude. To Mrs. Shirley Stewart, my mother-in-law ... my sister, Cassandra, and brother, Rodney... and grandfather, Charles, and other family and friends who have come, I say 'thank you' for sharing this day.

To the church officials and dignitaries, and the Board of Directors of the Multi-Ethnic Center for Ministry, I offer thanks to each of you for being here today. To the Center's past leadership – Dr. William B. McClain, Dr. Willard Williams, and Dr. William James, among others who have served the Multi-Ethnic Center and brought us to this point, I honor you. And to all of you, who love the church, I am honored and thankful that we can share in the blessing of this day.

I come today with profound humility given this opportunity to serve the church as the Executive Director of the Multi-Ethnic Center for Ministry. In beginning this journey, I have spent a great deal of time reflecting upon what it means to be called to ministry...how awesome a thought and experience this is.

I have thought back to my childhood in Washington, DC. Having lived the majority of my early years in a part of Washington called Anacostia, I have reflected on the realities of city life, and the realities facing the church, and the Northeastern Jurisdiction of United Methodism, as we move towards the new millennium.

For those who may know of Washington, DC, you may know that much of Anacostia now experiences the type of blight common in many urban areas today. You might know that drugs and violence, and various other signs of despair and death are the reality in many parts of Anacostia.

As I have reflected, my mind has wandered back to the days in which Christ lived... the communities in which Christ was reared. I can imagine Nazareth, the place where Christ grew to maturity, as a place that may have been much like the Anacostia(s) of today. The question that was on the minds of many concerning the Nazareth of Christ's day was, "Can anything good come out of Nazareth?" (John 1:46)

Considering the immensity of the problems facing Anacostia – and so many of our communities today – it is my sense that questions similar to those of the Lord's day are being asked. "Can anything good come out of the desolation, despair and destruction of the city?"

To shed light on this question, Dr. Harold Recinos offers insight on the stigma surrounding the town of Nazareth - and Galilee, the broader region – during the time that Jesus lived:

> Jesus comes from a part of the world rejected by the Jerusalem establishment (Nazareth of Galilee). Within the global and culturally diverse context of Galilee, Jesus directed his ministry toward those persons rejected by organized religion and neglected by society.
>
> Yet, this Galilean carpenter who walked with society's outcasts proceeds from the countryside toward Jerusalem, instructing people along the way about their oppression and turning away from God, directing attention to the kingdom of God (the realm of God) at hand.[1]

Can anything good come out of Nazareth? Can anything good emerge from our cities and counties in the global context of which we are a part today?

As the Multi-Ethnic Center for Ministry moves toward the 21st Century, I believe that tremendous opportunities await us as we seek to address these important questions. Ours is a vision to become a ministry of excellence and integrity. We will strive to build bridges among the various constituencies and ministries with which we serve throughout the church.

I am reminded of a comment shared by one of my teachers, Dr. William B. McClain almost 20 years ago in his Inaugural Address as the first Executive Director of the Multi-Ethnic Center: He said:

The Church of Wesley, with the largest ethnic minority membership of mainline Protestant Churches in America, has a unique opportunity to provide a forum for ethnic minorities to engage in a broadly inclusive pluralistic theological discussion.

One of the purposes of the Multi-Ethnic Center for Ministry is to initiate, encourage and promote that conversation among the minorities of America, and to make us more aware and able to participate in a world context with our brothers and sisters whose faith has been shaped and nurtured by their own cultural experience in Latin America, Africa, Asia, and the Pacific.[2]

As we gather today, I am convinced that God is calling the Multi-Ethnic Center, as a ministry of the United Methodist Church, to be Holy and Bold in its witness and service some twenty years after its inception. In this age of rapid change, God is calling us to a level of innovation, creativity, and relevance whereby our ministry engages in bringing about real change and growth in the lives of the people of our churches and communities.

As I reflect upon the various ethnic minority communities with which the Multi-Ethnic Center engages in ministry – those persons of Asian, Native American, Latino, and African descent – I am reminded of a symphony.

It has been suggested, "life is a symphony." The orchestra that produces the symphony is comprised of various musical instruments of diverse shapes, and a variety of sounds. While each instrument in the orchestra is quite different, each is important to the greater good of the symphony.

In fact, I suspect that it is of utmost concern to the conductor of the orchestra that each instrument, regardless of its apparent importance, or lack thereof, is properly tuned, lest it affect the quality of performance of the entire orchestra. Thus, each instrument is critical to the harmony and the production of a beautiful, melodious symphony.

Life is a symphony. I believe God calls us to continue to work towards harmony. When some among us are out of tune... when some of us hurt.... when some among us face the problem of racism daily ...when some of us struggle within the constraints of abject poverty at disproportionate rates ... the entire symphony is out of harmony.

In the midst of this symphony called life, God beckons us to work toward peace – the divine vision and hope of Shalom.

I am reminded of Dr. Martin Luther King's definition of peace. "True peace is not merely that absence of tension, but true peace is the presence of justice."

And so, how are we to live out the prophet Micah's vision of what God requires of us today? How will we "do justice, and love kindness, and walk humbly with the Lord our God." (Micah 6:8)

How will we live out the hope of the prophet Amos? That we – God's church – "let justice roll down as might, waters, and righteousness as an everflowing stream?" (Amos 5:24)

Today, we gather with these questions yet unanswered. But we also gather rejoicing in the hope that we share. We rejoice because of the opportunities that are before us to work for love, justice and peace.

We rejoice as we seek to participate in raising consciousness levels among the people called Methodist regarding issues of racial justice and economic opportunity.

We rejoice as we affirm Christ's vision that the Church

would practice radical inclusivity, as we work to better understand the church's universality in this expanding global village that is our world.

We rejoice that we have the opportunity, at the dawning of another Christian millennium, to participate in the critical work of developing the next generation of transformational, multicultural leaders, equipped to shepherd the church and society in this emerging post-modern world.

We rejoice that we have yet another opportunity to live out our founder John Wesley's hope and vision for the people called Methodist – that we would go forth in Holy Boldness, "reforming the nation and spreading Scriptural holiness."

I am persuaded today, that all these things are possible for the church. It is my pledge that with God's help, I will do all that is within my God-given ability to serve well in helping our church become stronger and more inclusive as we move ahead.

I invite you to partner with the Multi-Ethnic Center for Ministry as we embark upon this journey. Your prayers, participation, ideas, hopes, dreams, and guidance are welcome. Please join us as we strive to make this the ministry that God calls it to be.

We close with a final thought from Dr. William B. McClain who declared:

The Multi-Ethnic Center for Ministry must help the whole Church in its theological task – tap the streams which flow together at the deepest levels of our common humanity and needs.[3]

May God grant us the faith to persevere on the journey of reconciliation and restoration that is before us. May God grant us the wisdom and courage to recognize and affirm our differences. And may God grant us the love and grace to tap into those ever-flowing streams where we all discover our commonalities as children of the living Savior. Amen.

-Chapter 3-

REDEEMING THE DREAM: REVISITING DR. MARTIN LUTHER KING, JR.'S BELOVED COMMUNITY

(This lecture was first delivered at Shiloh Baptist Church in Washington, DC in February 2004, and was first published in the *African Heritage Theological Journal* in June 2004.)

This year we celebrate the 75th anniversary of the birth of Dr. Martin Luther King, Jr., the African American Baptist preacher from Georgia who shook the foundations of American Christendom. His faith in God is to be viewed as inseparable from the lessons of theology and fellowship that he taught, and the hope of *Beloved Community* that he perpetually sought to convey to all of humanity.

Blinded by parochial assumptions, many persons in America and abroad are often tempted to reduce and confine the rich complexity of King as a global-historical figure to the limits of quotations from a familiar speech. Without seeking to comprehend the depth and breadth of the man – the measure of his unique spiritual and intellectual giftedness - we tend to leave ourselves consistently at the point of simply quoting one of the lines from his famous "I Have a Dream" recitation delivered in our Nation's Capital in the summer of 1963.

Owing to the eloquence of King's words, it is easy for us to lose sight of his singular vision of *Beloved Community*. At the genesis of a new millennium, it is critical to recall and reclaim the prophetic vision of Martin Luther King, Jr. whose understanding of Christian faith led him to stand up against the most dominant and insipid social evils of his day – racism, classism and militarism (what he termed the "triplets of evil").

King's profound faith in God was rooted in notions of the human dignity (somebodyness) and the God-giftedness of all persons, and the equality that is inherent in all humanity. This faith was evident in King's indelible hope that we as a society – amidst the inexhaustible power of this God-giftedness, and despite the existential and communal fallenness that is most evidence in the perpetuation of the race (color) line and other forms of separation in America – possess the grace, if not yet the will, to overcome division, and move toward the realization of *Beloved Community*.

For King, if the church were to be the church, it would engage in a prophetic witness that would bring its spiritual, social, economic and political resources to bear in ways that would affirm God's love, and be truly reconciling, redeeming, liberating and transforming.

King's prophetic witness would spawn a religious and social movement unparalleled in American history. The demand for racial justice in the South would be the impetus for concomitant social and political movements across a number of sectors:

- The roots of the struggle for women's rights (feminism and womanism), the rights of gays and lesbians, the rights of workers and the disabled, and the rights of immigrants of various hews of brown, red, yellow and black can be traced to the prophetic stance of Dr. King.
- It was King who espoused a form of nonviolent social resistance that would ultimately lead to the passage of the Civil Rights Act (1964) and the Voting Rights Act (1965) by the Congress of the United States.
- The foundations of affirmative action – however we might view it today – is rooted in King's prophetic vision of equality and justice throughout society.
- The American Civil Rights movement - led by Dr. King - served as an impetus and model of liberation and human rights movements across the globe – in Africa, Asia, Europe, and Central and South America.

The great 20th century theologian, philosopher, pastor and mystic-prophet, Howard Thurman once stated, "any text without a context is a pretext." It is my observation that our collective attempts to comprehend and appropriate the work of Martin Luther King, Jr. has typically resulted in a pretext. Our attempts to know and relate with King, in historical perspective, have often resulted in persons taking his life and work out of context. We know of the "I Have a Dream" speech. We may even know that he was a minister, and some of us may know that he earned a Doctor of Philosophy degree in Systematic Theology from Boston University in 1955, at a time when the insipid nature of blatant overt racism – segregation, and jim/jane crow - continued to infect and afflict the United States in both the South and the North.

But too many persons - both white and black - continue to *caricature, canonize, and castigate* King without grappling with the full measure of the man. Few persons - in the church, the academy, and the general population - have sought to comprehend King and his life and work in its full context. Thus, King's life remains a pretext – waiting yet to be discovered, uncovered, unpacked, explicated, exegeted, and ultimately appropriated.

This essay will address Martin Luther King's conception of *Beloved Community,* with particular focus on ways that the church and society might seek to appropriate and re-appropriate his life and work within the context of 21st century – or postmodern - reality. This analysis entails three parts. First, a brief analysis of the spiritual and intellectual development of Martin Luther King, Jr. will be offered. Here the formative influences (roots) - familial, spiritual (the church), communal, and intellectual - on King's thought and praxis will be examined. Who and what in his early developmental years most influenced King? Secondly, some of the critical philosophical and practical aspects of King's framework of nonviolence, peacemaking, community-building, and racial reconciliation will be analyzed. How did the philosophical/ theological underpinnings of nonviolence (and nonviolent social resistance), and related concepts provide the framework (the fertile ground) for King's arrival at a vision of *Beloved Community?* Thirdly, notions of the Christian love ethic and *Beloved Community* as foundational for King's thought and praxis will be considered, with reflection on how *Beloved Community* might serve as the foundation for a model of reconciliation, peacemaking and community-building as we have now moved into the 21st century. What might the church – and the broader society today – glean from the life and ministry – the thought and practice (praxis) of King as we seek to actualize *Beloved Community* in the new millennium?

THE ROOTS OF MARTIN LUTHER KING, JR'S SPIRITUAL DEVELOPMENT

In order to comprehensively understand King's public achievement – as ultimately expressed in his appropriation of the notion of *Beloved Community* - it is critical to consider the early spiritual, social and psychological influences on his life.

Throughout his public life, Martin Luther King, Jr. consistently reached down into the deep streams of the religious experience and social integration that had been so integral to his early formation. It was within these streams that he seemed to consistently discover and re-discover the essence of a faithfulness in God, which would ultimately sustain him in his constant beckoning for persons in the church and society to heed the words of the Prophet Micah, to: "love kindness, and to do justice, and to walk humbly with God." (Micah 6:8) and the Prophet Amos, to: "Let justice roll down as waters, and righteousness as an ever-flowing stream." (Amos 5:24)

In most of the biographical works that have been written on Martin Luther King, Jr. over the past thirty years, a great deal of attention has been given to his intellectual development at Morehouse College in Atlanta, Crozer Theological Seminary in Philadelphia, and Boston University where he completed his doctoral studies. Certainly, his spiritual, emotional and intellectual development at these institutions, along with additional academic work at Harvard University and the University of Pennsylvania, provided the foundation for his intellectual public identity. These institutions provided the "fertile ground" necessary for progress in what King would refer to as "a serious intellectual quest for a method to eliminate social evil."

But in order to comprehend King's movement toward a theological praxis of nonviolent social resistance, his experiences and development at these institutions should be considered against the backdrop, and within the context of his earlier development.

There were three major influences present in King's early life that shaped his later attitudes and actions. These were:

(1) His black middle class family (which included his ex-

tended family and the family/community ethos in which
he was raised
(2) The religion of the Black Baptist church
(3) The patterns of racial segregation and discrimination
in the South.

Lewis V. Baldwin in *There is a Balm in Gilead,* suggests
that King's cultural roots were "folk, black, and southern." These
roots remained a part of King's thought and praxis throughout his
adult years.

Foundational to his early development were King's early
family experiences. In *Liberating Visions,* Robert Franklin suggests that King's fundamental character was shaped and nurtured
within the valuing context of the southern middle-class family structure. The Kings and Williamses were prominent leaders in the "new
South." His family tree included a long line of Baptist preachers
(his father, grandfather and great-grandfather were ministers), and
outspoken advocates for freedom and justice.

When he was very young, his parents noticed that M.L. (as
he was affectionately known) possessed an unusual ability to endure pain. Although obviously in pain during spankings, M.L. refused to cry. Franklin suggests that this ability to endure pain would
become evident again, as he would later face the injuries of American racism.

King's later views on racism in America can be clearly traced
to his early development. In his biography, *Let the Trumpet Sound,*
Stephen B. Oates reports on King's preschool years, when his closest playmate was a white boy whose father owned the store across
the street from the King family home. When the two friends entered school in 1935, they attended separate schools. One day, the
parents of his friend announced that M.L. could no longer play with
their son. Their explanation was, "Because we are white and you
are colored."

Later, around the dinner table, his parents responded to his
hurt by telling him the story of the black experience in America.
Oates points out that it was typically through conversations such as
this that black youth would be socialized into the protest traditions
of the black community and church.

MARTIN LUTHER KING, JR'S INTELLECTUAL DEVELOPMENT

King's early childhood experience with racism predisposed him to study and address the psychological and social effects of oppression. His later formal education was predicated upon and guided by the more informal learning and personal experience of his early years within the nurturing context of a close-knit family, church, and culture. These early influences are evident in the King's later intellectual attraction to:

(1) A model of the rational, black minister as organic intellectual as modeled by Benjamin E. Mays at Morehouse College and Mordecai Johnson at Howard University

(2) The model of nonviolent social transformation of Mohandas Gandhi, the Indian political/social reformer

(3) The philosophy of Personalism of Harold DeWolf and Edgar Brightman at Boston University

(4) The Christian Liberalism and Social Gospel of Walter Rauchenbusch

(5) The Christian Realism of Reinhold Niebuhr

(6) The Dialectical Method of Georg Wilhelm Friedrich Hegel

King's attraction to Dr. Benjamin Mays and other African American intellectuals and ministers was influenced by the early influence of his father, grandfather, and great-grandfather who were, before him, Baptist ministers. This model of ministry and intellectual engagement is rooted in the notion of what philosopher Cornell West refers to as the "organic intellectual."[4]   In contrast to the traditional western model of intellectual life where one's integration and intellectual development remains connected to academic life as a primary source and location - the "organic intellectual" remains connected to priestly (and other public) institutions (like the church and community).

King's intellectual life is thus to be primarily viewed in this organic, public context as exemplified by his ongoing connection to the Black Baptist church, the communities in which he would minister, and the public institutions such as the Southern Christian

Leadership Conference to which he would provide leadership. His attraction to the thought and praxis of Indian political/ social reformer Mohandas K. Gandhi can be traced to models of social activism and nonviolence inculcated throughout the southern Black church and culture during his youth, and especially in his early family life. Gandhi's sense of justice and passionate/prophetic stance for peace with justice (as exemplified in the Sanskrit concepts of ahimsa (non-injury) and Satyagraha (truth/love/soul force)) were values transmitted to King within the common ethos of his upbringing, as well as his later engagement with thinkers like Henry David Thoreau (*On the Duty of Civil Disobedience*).

King's attraction to the Personalism of L. Harold DeWolf and Edgar Sheffield Brightman, two of his professors during his doctoral studies at Boston University can be viewed within the context of a consistent striving to develop approaches to framing philosophical/theological conceptions of God, humanity, and the relations of humans to each other, to the world of nature, and to God.

King's consistent integration and appropriation of the liberal Social Gospel perspective of Walter Rauchenbusch with the Christian Realism of Reinhold Niebuhr can be viewed within the context of the complex nature of the southern black (often fundamentalist, yet liberation/justice-oriented) Christianity of King's upbringing in the Black Baptist Church.

King's appropriation of the Dialectical Method of G.W.F. Hegel can be seen in his constant attempt to arrive at a creative synthesis amidst the conflict, crisis and tension extant within the nature of humanity and society. This method would remain evident in the ongoing development of his conception of *Beloved Community*.

Each of these streams of philosophical and theological thought was consistently held in dialect throughout King's public ministry. Kenneth Smith and Ira Zepp, Jr., in their work on the thinking of Martin Luther King, suggest that these influences together provide critical insight into understanding King's persistent search for, and arrival at the notion of the "*Beloved Community*."

NOTION OF THE INTEGRATIVE PERSON

Critical to Martin Luther King, Jr.'s developing conception of *Beloved Community* was the notion of the *Integrative Person*. Robert L. Franklin offers the notion of the *Integrative Person* as that which best captures the essence Martin Luther King, Jr.'s ongoing development and thinking.[5]

In the summer of 1958, King was invited to deliver two devotional addresses at the first National Conference on Christian Education of the United Church of Christ at Purdue University. In one of his addresses, "The Dimensions of a Complete Life," he offered a vision of human fulfillment by using geometry as an organizing paradigm. King conceived the complete life to be a process, a quest, rather than an achievement.

Inspired by the geometric perfection of the New City of God (New Jerusalem) described in the Book of Revelation (chapter 21), King suggested that the complete life was analogous to a cube. Each of its three dimensions represents a significant individual commitment:

(1) The *length of life* corresponds to a person's inner concern for his or her own welfare and development (rational self-interest).

(2) The *breadth of life* corresponds to concern for the welfare of others (community).

(3) The *height of life* refers to concern for reconciliation and communion with God (divine relationship).

With regard to the notion of the length of life, King stressed:

"... is not its duration or its longevity, but it is the push forward to achieve life's personal ends and ambitions." It is the inward concern for a person's own welfare and the realization of his own purposes. The individual is concerned with developing his inner powers. It is that dimension of life in which the individual pursues personal ends and ambitions. King said, "Love yourself, if that means rational and healthy self-interest. You are commanded to do that."[6]

King pointed out that length without breadth, the second dimension of the complete life, is like a self-contained tributary having no outward flow to the ocean. Stagnant, still, and stale, it lacks both life and freshness.[7]   The "I" cannot attain fulfillment without the "thou." For its full development, the self needs other selves. Paul Tillich had observed that only a "thou" can make man realize he has an ego.[8] The breadth of life is that dimension of life in which we are concerned about others. An individual has not started living until one can rise above the narrow confines of individualistic concerns to the broader concerns of all humanity.

Finally, there is a third dimension, the height of life. King pointed out that some people never get beyond the first two dimensions, and thus life remains incomplete. They develop their inner powers, they love humanity, but they stop right there. Without God, even the most brilliant achievements on the other two dimensions soon prove to be empty and disillusioning. King pointed out that if persons are to live the complete life they must reach up and discover God.[9]

In challenging everyone to live an integrative life of *agape,* King developed the Christian implications of the second and third dimensions of the complete life and in effect maintained that at times the practice of *agape* may require suspension of the first dimension, immediate self-interest. As part of the challenge, he called for a "creative altruism" that makes concern for others the first law of life.   He indicated that Jesus had revealed the meaning of this altruism in his parable about the Good Samaritan who was moved by compassion to care for "a certain man" who had been robbed and beaten on the road to Jerico.[10]

King asserted that the altruism of the Samaritan was *universal, dangerous and excessive.*[11]   His altruism was *universal* since he did not seek to inquire into the nationality of the wounded man to determine whether he was a Samaritan or a Jew. He saw that he was "a certain man" in need, and that was sufficient for him to intervene. The Samaritan was a good neighbor who demonstrated dangerous and excessive altruism because, unlike the priest and the Levite who passed by the wounded man, he was willing to help any person in distress under any conditions, and he was able to look beyond external accidents to regard the stranger in need as his brother.

Jesus gave the command to love one's neighbor, and King explained that through this parable Jesus disclosed his definition of neighbor:

He is neither Jew nor Gentile; he is neither Russian nor American; he is neither Negro nor white. He is "a certain man" – any needy man – on one of the numerous Jerico roads of life.[12]

PHILOSOPHICAL FRAMEWORK OF NONVIOLENCE

The singular vision of Martin Luther King, Jr. was for the realization of *Beloved Community*. The means for the realization of such a vision was through nonviolent social resistance. King's theological project to link his conception of God-giftedness – as rooted in his early intellectual and spiritual development - to dialectical Christian praxis led him to call the Christian community to a form of sacrificial witness that would move persons of all races and nationalities beyond existing paradigms of ritual and theology, and toward authentic relationship.

Theologian James Cone speaks of the impact of Martin Luther King's prophetic witness in writing:

As a prophet, with a charisma never before witnessed in this century, King preached black liberation in the light of Jesus Christ and thus aroused the spirit of freedom in the black community. To be sure, one may argue that his method of nonviolence did not meet the needs of the black community in an age of black power; but it is beyond question that it was King's influence and leadership in the black community that brought us to the period in which we now live, and for that we are in debt. His life and message demonstrate that the "soul" of the black community is inseparable from liberation, but always liberation grounded in Jesus Christ...[13]

While rooted in the church, Martin Luther King, Jr.'s philosophy of nonviolence was derived from numerous other sources, as well. King received early exposure to civil disobedience by observing and hearing about the defiance of black people in Southern communities who refused to conform to Jim Crow laws. Later, he found in Henry David Thoreau a model and language to legitimate the practice before the dominant culture. He possessed firsthand knowledge of the social and political power of the Christian church and found in Walter Rauschenbusch a more complete elaboration of the prophetic and redemptive social mission of the church. As a sensitive and observant youth, he had learned that social change always entails conflict, and in the philosophy of Georg Wilhelm Friedrich Hegel he discovered the dialectical analysis of history that reinforced his faith and hope in the future. Although he had observed examples of social evil all of his life, King found in Reinhold Niebuhr a biblically informed theological analysis of collective sin and evil. Indeed, this understanding of the logic and rhythm of King's informal and formal learning can be applied to all of the major sources he embraced in shaping his own eclectic moral philosophy.[14] Although King learned much about the power of self-discipline and nonviolence from his father and extended family, Mohandas Gandhi embodied the ideal of nonviolence in a socially transformative manner.

Nonviolence played a critical role in the thinking and practice of Martin Luther King, Jr., and was integral to the Montgomery Movement, which began with the bus boycott in 1955, captured the fancy and support of the nation and much of the world. It would serve as the impetus for King's theo-praxis of nonviolent social resistance. What had begun as a demonstration for a better form of segregation (first-come-first-serve basis) developed under King's skillful and charismatic leadership into a holy cause. What was aimed at a week's duration stretched into 381 days of "tired feet and rested souls."

The philosophy of nonviolent social resistance contained several elements that King would continue to develop throughout his ministry, and which were codified into a set of principles in his first book *Stride Toward Freedom* in 1958.[15] An analysis of King's thinking indicates six general characteristics of nonviolent resistance as a means of protest and community-building.

1. *It must be emphasized that nonviolent resistance is not a method for passive cowards (It is conceived as a method of active resistance).*

2. *Nonviolent resistance does not seek to defeat or humiliate the opponent, but to win his friendship and understanding.*
3. *The attack is directed against forces of evil rather than against persons who happen to be doing evil.*
4. *There must be a willingness to accept suffering without retaliation, to accept blows from the opponent without striking back (redemptive suffering).*
5. *Nonviolent resistance avoids not only external physical violence, but also internal violence of the spirit.*
6. *Nonviolent resistance is based on the conviction that the universe is on the side of justice.*

First, according to King, *it must be emphasized that nonviolent resistance is not a method for passive cowards*; it was conceived by King and those who were a part of the Civil Rights movement as a method of active resistance. Persons were not to engage in nonviolent resistance because they were afraid or merely because of a lack of the instruments of violence. Mohandas Gandhi often said that if cowardice is the only alternative to violence, it is better to fight. He made this statement conscious of the fact that there is always another alternative to violence. Nonviolence is ultimately the way of the strong person.

A second basic characteristic of nonviolent resistance, according to King, is that *it does not seek to defeat or humiliate the opponent, but to win his friendship and understanding.* In this regard, King stated:

The nonviolent resister most often expresses his protest through non-cooperation or boycotts, but he realizes that these are not ends themselves; they are merely means to awaken a sense of moral shame in the opponent. The end is redemption and reconciliation. The aftermath of nonviolence is the creation of the *Beloved Community*, while the aftermath of violence is tragic bitterness.

A third characteristic of this method is that *the attack is directed against forces of evil rather than against persons who happen to be doing evil.* Regarding this distinction, King pointed out:

It is evil that the nonviolent resister seeks to defeat, not the persons who are the perpetrators of evil. If one is opposing racial injustice, the nonviolent resister has the vision to see that the basic tension is not between the persons of different races.

A fourth characteristic of nonviolent resistance is *a willingness to accept suffering without retaliation, to accept blows from the opponent without striking back.* Here, King refers to the thinking of Mohandas Gandhi to make his point about the suffering of the resister:

Gandhi said to his countrymen, "Rivers of blood may have to flow before we gain freedom, but it must be our blood." The nonviolent resister is willing to accept violence if necessary, but never to inflict it. He does not seek to dodge jail if going to jail is necessary to meet the objectives of social change through nonviolence.

The nonviolent resister's justification (rationale) for this is found in the notion that unearned suffering is redemptive. The nonviolent resister realizes that suffering has tremendous educational and transformational possibilities. Gandhi said:

Things of fundamental importance to people are not secured by reason alone, but have to be purchased with their suffering.... Suffering is infinitely more powerful than the law of the jungle for converting the opponent and opening his ears which are otherwise shut to the voice of reason.

Martin Luther King, Jr. suggests that a fifth characteristic of nonviolent resistance is that *it avoids not only external physical violence but also internal violence of the spirit.* The nonviolent resister not only refuses to shoot his opponent, but he also refuses to hate him. At the center of nonviolence stands the principle of love. King elaborates on love as central to nonviolence:

The nonviolent resister would contend that in the struggle for human dignity, the oppressed people of the world must not succumb to the temptation of becoming bitter or indulging in hate campaigns. To retaliate in kind would do nothing but intensify the existence of hatred in the universe. Along the way of life, someone must have sense enough and morality enough to cut off the chain of hate. This can only be done by projecting the ethic of love to the center of our lives.

In speaking of love at this point, we are not referring to some sentimental and affectionate emotion. It would be nonsense to urge persons to love oppressors in an affectionate sense. Love in this context means understanding, redemptive goodwill. Here the Greek language comes to our aid. There are three words for love in the Greek New Testament. First, there is *eros*. In platonic philosophy *eros* meant the yearning of the souls for the realm of the divine. It has come now to mean a sort of aesthetic or romantic love. Second is *philia*, which means intimate affection between personal friends. *Philia* denotes a sort of reciprocal love; the person loves because he is loved. When we speak of loving those who oppose us, we refer to neither *eros* nor *philia;* we speak of a love that is expressed in the Greek word *agape. Agape* means understanding, redeeming goodwill for all men. It is an overflowing love, which is purely spontaneous, unmotivated, groundless, and creative. It is not set in motion by any quality or function of its object. It is the love of God operating in the human heart.

King points out that a sixth characteristic of nonviolent resistance is that *it is based on the conviction that the universe is on the side of justice.* With regard to this, King says:

Consequently, the believer in nonviolence has deep faith in the future. This faith is another reason why the nonviolent resister can accept suffering without retaliation. For he knows that in his struggle for justice, he has cosmic companionship. It is true that there are devout believers in nonviolence who find it difficult to believe in a personal God. But even those persons believe in the existence of some creative force that works for universal wholeness. Whether we call it an unconscious process, an impersonal Brahman, or a Personal Being of matchless power and infinite love, there is a creative force in this universe that works to bring the disconnected aspects of reality into a harmonious whole.

TOWARDS THE CHRISTIAN LOVE-ETHIC AND THE SEARCH FOR *BELOVED COMMUNITY*

Kenneth Smith and Ira Zepp, Jr. in *Search for the Beloved Community,* suggest that Martin Luther King, Jr.'s perspective on the Christian love-ethic provides critical insight into understanding his persistent search for the *"Beloved Community."*[16] A recurring theme in King's sermons, throughout his career, was what he called *Beloved Community.* It was rooted in the biblical notion of *Agape* (God's unconditional love), and was the ultimate goal for which he worked.

In King's conception of *Beloved Community,* faith and action were interrelated. In this regard, King viewed theology and ethics as inextricably connected. Theology – what we believe and comprehend about God (how we talk about God), could not be separated from ethics - who we are, and what we do as the human family. Our creed and our deed had to be in concert. Our talk and our walk had to correspond.

This faith-action (creed-deed) dialectic found its ultimate expression in the notion of *Beloved Community.* For King, there were two steps involved in the movement towards *Beloved Community.* (1) *Desegregation* would lead to the removal of legal barriers to equality. But desegregation was a short-term goal – and it alone was not enough. Desegregation had to be followed by *integration.* (2) *Integration* advocated and facilitated the inclusion of all persons in a just society. King defined integration as genuine inter-group, interpersonal living. Integration was the long-term goal as a means toward realizing the vision of *Beloved Community.*

For King, the *Beloved Community* was an integrated community in which persons of all races and creeds lived together harmoniously as sisters and brothers in peace. It was the Kingdom of God on earth. King stated, "I do not think of political power as an end. Neither do I think of economic power as an end. They are ingredients in the objective we seek in life. And I think that end, that objective, is a truly brotherly society, the creation of *Beloved Community*."[17]

In the final analysis, Martin Luther King, Jr. asserted that "all life is interrelated." One of his fundamental beliefs was the kinship of all persons. He believed all life is part of a single process; all living things are interrelated; and all persons are sisters and brothers. All have a place in the *Beloved Community*. Because all are interrelated, one cannot harm another without harming oneself. King said:

> To the degree that I harm my brother, no matter what he is doing to me, to that extent I am harming myself. For example, white men often refuse federal aid to education in order to avoid giving the Negro his rights; but because all men are brothers they cannot deny Negro children without harming themselves. Why is this? Because all men are brothers. If you harm me, you harm yourself. Love, *agape*, is the only cement that can hold this broken community together. When I am commanded to love, I am commanded to restore community, to resist injustice, and to meet the needs of my brothers.[18]

The quest for the *Beloved Community* – through *Agape* - would lead King to take a consistently prophetic stance against the powerfully regressive ideological apparatus of the Jim Crow racism of the Southern church and society, and the more apathetic, sophisticated brand of racism experienced in the North.

When the Montgomery Bus Boycott ended, Martin Luther King, Jr. spoke at a victory rally on December 3, 1956. He pointed out that the goal had not been to defeat other persons, but to awaken the conscience of others to challenge the false sense of superiority that persons might harbor. Now that victory had been achieved, King said, it was time for reconciliation. "The end is reconciliation; the end is the creation of *Beloved Community*."

Conclusion

Today, it is in the affirmation of the God-giftedness of all humanity, as manifest in the perpetual striving toward *Beloved Community*, through the appropriation of the Christian love-ethic (agape love), that the church and society can begin to constructively address disintegration and disunity such as racism and its concomitant evils - economic deprivation and military annihilation - that continue to serve as hindrances to true peace and authentic community.

Martin Luther King, Jr. said that "true peace is not merely the absence of tension – true peace is the presence of justice." King's vision of *Beloved Community* was rooted in justice. Without justice, there was no possibility of the realization of authentic, peaceful community.

Like Jesus Christ in the temple that had become a den of thieves, King realized that the church and society are fertile grounds for corruption, evil and injustice. King's belief remained that God, as radically and actively involved agape love in action, seeking the freedom and justice of humanity, was, in the final analysis, working toward universal wholeness and the restoration of justice and *Beloved Community*.

-Chapter 4 -

PIECES OF A DREAM

(This sermon was first delivered at Ames United Methodist Church in Bel Air, MD. in 1996.)

Once Joseph had a dream, and when he told his brothers, they hated him even more. He said to them, "Listen to this dream that I dreamed. There we were, binding sheaves in the field. Suddenly my sheaf rose and stood upright; then your sheaves gathered around it, and bowed down to my sheaf." His brothers said to him, "Are you indeed to reign over us? Are you indeed to have dominion over us?" So they hated him even more because of his dreams and his words. (Genesis 37:5-8)

The fragmentation of our days is clearly evident in the various forms of societal decay and despair that is our reality today. We are fragmented in many ways. AIDS and HIV continue to afflict too many in our community and across the globe. Crack cocaine and heroine are still endemic to too many of our neighborhoods.

Too many persons are uneducated, undereducated, unemployed, underemployed, incarcerated, adjudicated, homeless, helpless, hapless and apparently hopeless.

We are fragmented by racism, colorism, sexism, classism, elitism, materialism and denominationalism. We are fragmented by war, terror, violence, the misogyny of our women, the hate of our men, and the neglect of our children. We are fragmented by isolation, alienation, discrimination, separation, and segregation.

Joseph was a dreamer. Joseph dreamt of opportunities and possibilities that seemed to be beyond his present reality. And as is the case with many dreamers, Joseph found himself in discord with those who were the closest to him. Joseph found himself in the precarious position of being hated and despised by some of the very persons who were supposed to love him and support him the most.

Joseph was a dreamer. And it was his brothers who seemed

to find it the most difficult to understand Joseph and his dreaming. Joseph was thinking too big. He was considered to be unrealistic at the least, and arrogant at the worst. (Who did Joseph think he was, to be dreaming like he was?)

And so his brothers set out to get rid of Joseph, and his dream.

We are reminded that when we find ourselves dreaming, we may encounter circumstances, obstacles and stumbling blocks similar to those that Joseph encountered. When we dream, we will discover that there will be persons who don't dream as we dream - and think our dreams to be ludicrous and outlandish. There will invariably be some people who will try to kill the dreams of any dreamer.

But what dreamers need to be cognizant of is that dreams are an indelible part of any faith journey. That is what would lead the prophet Joel to declare that: "In the last days God would pour out God's Spirit on all flesh - and older persons would dream dreams, and younger persons will see visions." (Joel 2:28)

What Joel was trying to say about dreams is that dreams are critical to persons of faith remembering their past, and seeing their future. We must have some dreamers among us in order to live into the future. We must have some dreamers among us in order to hope and to see the possibilities that are before us. We must have some people who are willing and able to dream in order to see beyond what the circumstances are – or appear to be – to what God has in store for God's people.

Today, God needs just a few people who are willing to dream so that they can help the church and society look beyond and live beyond - the hopelessness and despair, the muck and the mire of this present day. God needs some dreamers today.

There is a need for dreamers, for when we fail to dream, we cash in our future to despair. When we fail to dream, we succumb to dread and hopelessness. When we fail to dream, we inevitably will die.

One of the problems with the church and the world today is that there are not enough people who are willing to dream. Too many people have conformed to the ways of the world, and have forgotten how to lift up their heads and hearts to see what God would dare to do with our lives in this present day.

Martin Luther King, Jr., like Joseph, was a dreamer. Dr. King dared to dream, and invited others to dream with him. He dreamt a world of peace with justice – a world where "justice would roll down as waters, and righteousness as an ever-flowing stream." (Amos 5:24) Dr. King dreamt a world where people would love kindness, and do justice and walk humbly with God. (Micah 6:8)

Dr. King dreamt a world devoid of racism and segregation – a world where all children would be educated, all persons would have access to adequate healthcare and good employment. He dreamt a world where all persons would be fed and housed and cared for.

And as with Joseph, there were those who sought to destroy Martin Luther King's dream – and not only destroy his dream – but destroy the dreamer.

And so it is today, many people wonder whether or not Dr. King's dream continues to live, or whether his dream has become a nightmare. I'd venture to suggest that although Dr. King's dream has not been completely fulfilled, as we look around, we witness signs that his dream is yet alive.

We see pieces of a dream.
• There have been gains in the black and brown middle class in America.
• More women of all races serve in roles of leadership in the church, and across society than at any other time in the history of our nation.
• More black and brown persons have college degrees, own homes, and work in professions than at any other time in our nation's history.

These are pieces of Dr. King's dream.

But for Dr. King's dream and our dreams to be completely realized, I believe we must be intentional, persistent and faithful about continuing to add pieces to our collective dreams. We as a church and society must think, pray, and act locally and globally in courageous and creative ways to eradicate racism, poverty and war in our lifetime. We must continue to close societal gaps in income, wealth, employment, education, health-care, housing and technology among people.

How might we dare to dream and make a difference in this present day?

What we realize is that what really helped Martin Luther King, Jr. dream dreams, was that he had gotten to know another dreamer. It's good to know that Dr. King knew a dreamer named Jesus.

The Scriptures tell us that Jesus was a dreamer. The Lord dreamt a world where:
Captives would be set free
The blind would see
The lame would walk
And the poor would receive some good news.
(Luke 4:18-19)

Jesus dreamt a world where:
Every valley would be exalted
And every hill and every mountain made low.
The crooked made straight,
And rough places made plain.
And the glory of the Lord would be revealed.
(Isaiah 40:4-5)
I'm glad that Jesus dreamt dreams, and saw visions.

Because he dreamed, we can dream today.

Because he lives, we can face tomorrow
Because he lives, all fear is gone.
Because we know, who holds the future,
Life is worth the living....
Just because he lives.

-Chapter 5 -

IN TRIBUTE TO
DR. MARTIN LUTHER KING, JR.

A TEN POINT ACTION PLAN
FOR UNITED METHODISTS

(This was first published as an article in the *West Virginia United Methodist* in February 2000, and was also published in the *United Methodist Connection of the Baltimore-Washington Conference*.)

During his life, Dr. Martin Luther King believed that everyone could be great because everyone could serve. Making a sincere commitment to the King holiday and all it represents, as well as taking some appropriate action to serve the causes of equality, justice, freedom and peace, are ways in which individuals, churches, groups, organizations, institutions and even governments can act to continue Dr. King's unfinished work, and to perpetuate the pursuit of his vision of the Beloved Community.

Here are ten ways that we can act to honor the dream and legacy of Dr. King:

1. Support and develop community-wide plans aimed at expanding economic opportunities for racial-ethnic persons and women specifically in the areas of housing, banking and employment practices.

2. Plan to actively participate in an event that reaches out to those in the most need – the hungry, the homeless and the unemployed.

3. Adopt an inner-city school. Offer your skills where appropriate. Do your part to assure that every inner city young person can look

forward to an adequate education.

4. Encourage schools, colleges and universities in your community to include Dr. King's teachings in their curricula and programs.

5. Take specific actions to deal with the problems of drugs, alcohol dependency, teenage pregnancy, and family violence.

6. Become an advocate - and encourage church, political and community leaders to advocate - for the removal of all weapons from our streets, homes and schools.

7. Support causes that promote freedom, justice and peace abroad. Help extend human rights, dignity, health and economic well-being to all persons.

8. Take a stand, and encourage persons in your church and community to actively oppose those groups that promote hatred and violence. Actively and vigilantly oppose racism, homophobia and other forms of xenophobia in our communities.

9. Sponsor and participate in programs that encourage interracial and intercultural goodwill and unity.

10. Read the Social Principles of The United Methodist Church, and strive to make them an integral part of the faith and life of yourself and your church.

-Chapter 6 -

UP CLOSE AND PERSONAL: THE SEARCH FOR PEACEFUL COMMUNITY

(This sermon was first delivered at a Black History Month worship celebration at Wesley Theological Seminary in Washington, DC in February 2000).

"The wolf shall dwell with the lamb, the leopard shall lie down with the kid, the calf and the lion and the fatling together, and a child shall lead them." (Isaiah 11:6)

One of the critical components of the adventure of discipleship is fellowship. For the church, fellowship speaks to the ways that we as Christians live into becoming authentic community. As a way of visualizing community, author and professor Eric Law, in his book *The Wolf Shall Dwell with the Lamb,* offers the image of the wolf and the lamb dwelling together in peace and harmony. Though different in disposition and character, the wolf and the lamb, through a common spirit learn to peaceably co-exist because it is in their interests to live together.

This was the vision of the biblical prophet Isaiah – a vision in which the wolf and the lamb would dwell together peaceably. *"The wolf shall dwell with the lamb, the leopard shall lie down with the kid, the calf and the lion and the fatling together, and a child shall lead them." (Isaiah 11:6)* Amidst the turmoil, pestilence and virulence that had become so much a part of Israel's existence, it was Isaiah's prophetic vision of a peaceable realm, where persons who differed would exist together in life and living. Isaiah's was a vision rooted in the hope that God would do what people had been - to that point - unable to do on their own. It was a vision where God would move persons toward the realization of true community – where swords would be turned into plowshares, and spears into pruning hooks, where God would facilitate peace among persons and nations, and where persons would study war no more. (Isaiah 2:4)

To understand Isaiah's vision of the peaceable realm, we have to first sense the very nature of God. God is shalom. Walter Bruegemmann, among other biblical theologians, offers that the very nature of God is shalom – peace, wholeness, health and well-being. God desires – God wills - shalom for all of humanity. Violence and war, and even many of the social distinctions that serve to separate persons - race, gender, economic and class structures, along with the ways that we tend to separate ourselves religiously - can be viewed as antithetical to God's will – to shalom – if they separate us and do not facilitate community.

I sense that this search for peace and community – this yearning for shalom - has been one of the most consistent strivings among humans over the course of history. The psalmist encouraged us to "seek peace and pursue it." (Psalm 34:14) And in another place the psalmist exclaimed, "how good and pleasant it is when persons live together in unity." (Psalm 133:1)

It has been persons like Howard Thurman, Martin Luther King, Jr., Mohandas Gandhi, Mother Theresa, Rosa Parks, Oscar Romero, Thomas Merton, and Henri Nouwen, who have helped us in the recent past to not forget this constant striving, this common thirst for peace. They, among many others chose the radical way of peace, demonstrating that to choose peace is to live in the will of God. To choose peace is to draw closer to God and to one another. And each of them showed us that peace must always be connected with justice. Martin Luther King, Jr. reminded us, that "true peace is not merely the absence of tension; it is the presence of justice."

In this postmodern reality, to radically choose peace begins by seeing violence as the common concern of all who are the church and society. Regardless of our geographic or social location, we are all affected by the proliferation – the very permeation - of violence in our midst. Whether in our schools, in our homes, or on our jobs, we are all affected. Whether violence is manifest through our actions, our words or our thoughts, we are all commonly affected.

And so God beckons us to make the radical choice to live in peace. To be the church and society is to be in relationships that are up close and personal with those who may appear to be different than we are. It is to actively seek to understand, and to come to value the lives of those who are the "others" among us. In *The Mood of Christmas,* Howard Thurman intimated, "Despite my tendency to feel my race superior, my nation the greatest nation, my faith the true faith, I must beat down the boundaries of my exclusiveness until my sense of separateness is completely enveloped in a sense of fellowship.[19]

This up close and personal reality that is the way of peace will lead us - from time to time - to go out on a limb in our faith journey. Are we willing to go out on a limb for what we believe?

I am reminded of the man who found himself falling over the edge of a cliff one day. As he was falling, the man was able to grab the limb of a tree, and hang on for dear life. As he held on, he looked down, and he realized how far down it was to jump. And so he looked up, and began to talk to God. "God, are you up there? And if you are, please tell me what to do." God responded to the man, and said, "If you trust me, just let go." The man looked down again, and then he looked back up, and asked, "Is there anybody else up there?"

Are we willing to go out on a limb for what we believe? Are willing to go out on a limb for Jesus? This is necessary if we are to live lives that are up close and personal. This is lived out as we continue to be commonly concerned about each other's well-being.

In one of his noted sermons, Martin Luther King, Jr., recounted the story of the time that he was stabbed with a letter opener, and found himself on the brink of death. Physicians worked feverishly and faithfully to save his life, and he was able to escape death. As he lay in the recovery room, one of the physicians came by and talked to King. The physician informed King how very close he had come to actually dying. Martin Luther King, Jr. learned that the letter opener was lodged in a way that if he had sneezed, the letter opener would have severed his aorta and he would have died. If he had sneezed...

In the aftermath of this terrible experience, Dr. King received a letter from a young girl whom he had never met. He discovered later that she was a little white girl. In her letter, the little girl wrote, "Dr. King, I'm writing to tell you how sorry I am that you got stabbed, but I also want you to know that I'm glad that you didn't sneeze."

Isaiah ends his vision of "wolves and lambs dwelling together" with another radical notion, "and a little child shall lead them."

How radical is our yearning for peace? How are we concerned for the well-being of our neighbors? With whom does God call us to relate in up close and personal ways? How are we willing to go out on a limb for Christ? "And a little child shall lead them."

Living in an up close and personal manner may require of us a childlike faithfulness – not unlike the little girl who wrote to Martin Luther King, Jr. It will certainly require of us that we seek to "love kindness and to do justice and to walk humbly with God." (Micah 6:8) And it will lead us to envision, imagine, hope and dream of a future where we celebrate the common giftedness that we share as God's fearfully and wonderfully created children.

Langston Hughes shared such a dream in a poem:

I dream a world where man
No other man will scorn,
Where love will bless the earth
And peace its paths adorn.
I dream a world where all
Will know sweet freedom's way,
Where greed no longer saps the soul
Nor avarice blights our day.
A world I dream where black or white,
Whatever race you be,
Will share the bounties of the earth
And every man is free,
Where wretchedness will hang its head
And joy, like a pearl
Attends the needs of all mankind –
Of such I dream my world!

NOTES ON SECTION ONE

[1] Harold J. Recinos, *Jesus Weeps: Global Encounters on our Doorstep.* (Nashville: Abingdon Press, 1997, pp. 45-46).
[2] William B. McClain, *Black People in the Methodist Church: Wither Thou Goest?* (Nashville: Abingdon Press, 1984, p.131). Dr. McClain made this comment at his installation service as the first Executive Director of the Multi-Ethnic Center for Ministry of the United Methodist Church. The sermon was entitled, "Strangers at Home."
[3] Ibid., 132.
[4] Cornel West, *Prophetic Fragments: Illuminations of the Crisis in American Religion and Culture* (Grand Rapids, MI: Reedman's, 1988), 3.
[5] Martin Luther King, Jr., "Three Dimensions of the Complete Life," in *Strength to Love* (New York: Harper and Row, 1963), 69-73.
[6] Kenneth Smith and Ira Zepp, *Search for Beloved Community* (Valley Forge: Judson Press, 1974), 76.
[7] Ibid., 71.
[8] See, Robert Franklin, *Liberating Visions,* 109f. Franklin points out that King, in his conception of the "Three Dimensions of the Complete Life," makes reference to Paul Tillich, *Love, Power and Justice,* (London: Oxford University Press, 1954), 78.
[9] King, "Three Dimensions of the Complete Life," *Strength to Love,* 69-73.
[10] John J. Ansbro, *Martin Luther King, Jr.: Nonviolent Strategies and Tactics for Social Change* (Maryknoll, NY: Orbis Books, 2000), 30.
[11] King, *Strength to Love,* 17-24.
[12] Ibid., 17.
[13] James Cone, *A Black Theology of Liberation,* 37.
[14] Franklin, 108-109.
[15] King, *Stride Toward Freedom: The Montgomery Story*

(New York: Harper and Row, 1958). In this work Martin Luther King, Jr. outlines his doctrine of nonviolence.

[16] Smith and Zepp, in *Search for the Beloved Community,* the matter of King's development of the concept of *Beloved Community* within the context of the Christian love- ethic is explicated at various points throughout the book.

[17] Martin Luther King, Jr., in *The Christian Century,* (Chicago, IL: Christian Century, July 13, 1966).

[18] King, "Loving Your Enemies," *Strength to Love,* 41-50.

[19] Howard Thurman, *The Mood of Christmas* (Richmond, IN: Friends United Press, 1973), 19-20.

SECTION TWO

- Chapter 7 -

A PRAYER FOR INTERFAITH UNITY (IN THE AFTERMATH OF 9-11)

(This was the Opening Prayer for the Harford County, MD Human Relations Commission, Interfaith Prayer Service in the Aftermath of the Terrorist Attacks of September 11, 2001, delivered on October 4, 2001 at New Hope Baptist Church, Bel Air, MD. Persons from the Islamic, Jewish, Ba'hai, Unitarian Universalist and Christian faith communities shared in this Prayer Service.)

It has been said, "a thinker thrives in the rough current that pushes
    against her/him."
God, creator of all the earth, and all faith
    God of Mecca and Jerusalem,
      God of New York and Washington, DC and
        Pennsylvania and Virginia
We now look to you in these moments of uncertainty, fear and doubt.
As the dust is now settling, and we count the lost among us,
    We humbly beseech you,
      O God, to guide our thoughts and our emotions
        To temper our words and our actions in the days ahead.

As difficult as these days and weeks have been,
    We know that difficult days are yet ahead,
      And we pray - O God - for your abiding presence among us.
      We ask a particular blessing upon those family members
        and friends who have lost loved ones amidst the terror
        that we have all witnessed.
We offer thanksgiving - and our continual prayers for those who
    have provided rescue, recovery, care,
      and comfort amidst the tragedy.

We pray for a modicum of wisdom for the leaders of our nation
   and our world, as they contemplate the decisions
      that are before them.
         Guide our leaders toward those actions that are
         right and just in your sight.

O God we pray that you will make us instruments of peace.
Season our presence here (this evening) with a sense of unity and
   an appreciation of the commonalities that we share as the human
      family that in moments when we may feel the most
         separated from self, from one another, and even from you –
O God - you will make us ever mindful of your abiding presence.
      And even as we are now broken in so many ways,
         even amidst pain and disappointment, even amidst the
            bitter tears that have flowed so often,
            and in such immensity over these days,
We pray that you will heal the land,
      heal our hurts, and heal our relationships.
         And by your grace and mercy, make us forever mindful,
         that even in these rough currents that we now experience,
         You are God. Amen.

-Chapter 8-

THE CHURCH AND REPARATIONS: MORE THAN MONEY

(This essay was first published as an article in the *United Methodist Connection* of the Baltimore-Washington Conference in 2003. It was also published by the United Methodist News Service.)

What does the United States owe African-Americans? What does the United Methodist Church owe Black Methodists? It has been more than thirty years since black activist James Foreman walked down the aisle during the Sunday morning worship service of the largely white Riverside Church in New York City and read a *Black Manifesto* which called upon American churches and synagogues to pay $500 million as a "beginning of the reparations due us as people who have been exploited and degraded, brutalized, killed and persecuted."

Today, the debate about reparations continues to rage in academic and political circles. Richard America, a Georgetown University Professor estimates that U.S. government owes African-Americans five to ten trillion dollars for the slavery that persons were forced to endure. In the aftermath of the United Methodist Church's ritual acts of repentance and reconciliation at the 2000 General Conference, the matter of reparations as a possible constructive extension of these ritual acts is before the Church. The 2000 Northeastern Jurisdiction Conference commissioned a Task Force to study the effects of the 1968 merger on churches and related institutions that were a part of the former (all-black) Central Jurisdiction. The Task Force is to report its findings to the 2004 Jurisdictional Conference in Syracuse, New York.

Any discussion of reparations must begin by defining the term, and then determining within the context of the definition, whether or not reparations are warranted. Reparation can simply be defined as making amends for a wrong, injury or injustice. The philosopher Plato asserted that justice exists when persons get what they deserve. Injustice, therefore, exists when and where people do not get what they deserve.

In the case of Blacks in America, a preponderance of evidence leads to the conclusion that slavery, and subsequent forms of Jim and Jane Crow, have resulted in injury and injustice to African-Americans. This injustice is evidenced in the death of millions of Africans during the Middle Passage; the systematic disintegration of black families through separation of family members from one another; and the economic oppression incumbent in slavery where Blacks were treated not as humans, but as chattel property, and never compensated for labor which, in large measure has served as the foundation of America's system of capitalism.

Furthermore, many would argue that the legacy of slavery has continued to plague African Americans. Philosopher Cornel West places this legacy within the context of what he terms the "nihilism of Black America." According to West, this nihilism exists as a certain nothingness - a meaninglessness and lovelessness - that continues to plague much of black life in America. This nihilism is evident in disproportionate rates of poverty, addictive behaviors, family dysfunction, poor health, and violence in black communities, a well as the relatively low level of academic achievement among many black youth, especially in urban areas.

Given the legacy of racism in America, the question remains one of what - if anything - does the U.S. owe African-Americans? Thinkers like Randall Robinson (Pan Africa), Charles J. Ogletree (a law professor at Harvard University), and nationally noted attorney Johnnie Cochran assert that indeed America owes African-Americans for the rich history that slavery and segregation severed. They argue that white Americans can begin making reparations for slavery and the century of *dejure* discrimination that followed with monetary restitution, educational programs, and the kinds of equal opportunities that will ensure the social and economic success of all citizens. Their argument for reparations is based on the notion that there has been damage that has occurred, and that this damage can and should somehow be remedied.

In many ways, the effects of slavery and segregation continue to persist in the church, as well as in society. In fact, the vast majority of United Methodist congregations remain essentially seg-regated. In the church, the effects of America's racist legacy are evident in the decline of many of mainline black churches - includ-ing numerous United Methodist congregations. Over the past thirty years - this decline is apparent in consistent decreases in member-ship, attendance, stewardship, and diminished vitality in worship and witness in many churches.

In 1968, at the dawn of the formation of the United Meth-odist Church and the elimination of the former Central Jurisdiction, Martin Luther King, Jr. eloquently and prophetically cautioned that with the elimination of the Central Jurisdiction, there existed the possibility of Black Methodists "being integrated out of power." Some thirty-five years later we are left to ponder the profundity and accuracy of Dr. King's observation.

For the Christian church, a biblical-theological concern with regard to reparations is rooted in a question raised by the prophet Ezekiel in the 6th century B.C.E. "Who will stand in the breach?" "I looked for anyone among them who would repair the wall and stand in the breach...but I found no one." (Ez. 22:30)

Is there a way for the church to equitably share power and resources? What will ecumenism and evangelism across racial lines look like, given the cultural and theological differences that are among us? How is wholeness and healing to occur amidst the vari-ous perspectives that have emerged with regard to reparations? Is it possible for Christians to engage in authentic ritual acts of repen-tance and reconciliation without simultaneously developing means of reparation and renewal?

A constructive approach to standing in the breach and re-storing hope for persons in the church and society might begin with a systematic restructuring of the socio-political landscape in America. A more just distribution of the essential political goods of society - education, employment, health-care, housing, safety, technology and transportation- would offer clear evidence of this systematic restruc-turing.

As we stand in the breach within the church, we might de-velop strategic approaches to refurbishing older decaying church buildings inherited by black congregations as many whites who for-merly worshipped in urban churches now reside and worship in the relative comfort of the suburbs. We might develop approaches and commit adequate resources aimed at the wholistic education of the young, and the spiritual, emotional and physical care and empowerment of the dispossessed and distressed. In standing in the breach, the Christian church might create effective models of economic and community development, leading to the creation of more jobs that pay living wages, the construction of affordable homes, and the building of state-of-the-art schools.

As we stand in the breach, we who are United Methodists might seek to realistically unite with our sisters and brothers who are African Methodist Episcopal, African Methodist Episcopal Zion and Christian Methodist Episcopal. Each of us might seek to authentically relate – through worship, fellowship, and service - with Christians who are culturally and ethnically different from us.

It appears that a part of our theological task is to stand in the breach. May God grant us the wisdom, compassion and courage to do what is just and right in God's sight.

-Chapter 9–

THE AFFIRMATIVE ACTION
DEBATE OUT OF FOCUS

(This essay was published as an article in the *United Methodist Connection* of the Baltimore-Washington Conference in September 1995. At the time, the author was the pastor of Ames UMC in Bel Air, MD).

The recent public debate over whether or not affirmative action should be repealed – or at the least scaled back – has several underlying issues that are seldom discussed, but are – in large measure – driving the debate.

Those who have argued the most fervently against affirmative action seem to be constantly striving towards driving home the notion that people of color and women are inherently inferior to white males in many respects, and thus do not deserve whatever measure of access and success that they have attained.

We know this not to be the case, as many blacks and women in management and executive level positions in the work place are generally better qualified in terms of education and experience than their white male counterparts in similar jobs.

Additionally, the debate on comparable worth for minorities and women seems to have died in the midst of the affirmative action debate, as minorities and women generally continue to receive considerably less compensation for doing the same jobs.

Furthermore, it is clear that the proverbial "glass ceiling" continues to exist for most ethnic persons and women in the work place as these groups are significantly under-represented in higher level executive positions - despite education and experience – in both the private and public sectors.

It is tragic that this has become a debate focused primarily on race gender and quotas instead of fair access to employment, education, and other opportunities – which was the original intent of affirmative action. History shows us that the overriding intent of Martin Luther King, Jr., Thurgood Marshall and other champions of civil rights throughout the 1950's and '60's was not that marginalized persons would be privy to various and sundry set-asides and quotas, but that all persons would have equal and fair access to every aspect of American society, from education, to employment, to housing, to politics. The premise here is that fairness and equality in all sectors is essential to justice and peace, and leads to a better society for all.

Affirmative action is not simply about giving minorities preference in the various sectors of economic activity. Affirmative action is about leveling the playing field for persons of all colors, cultures, genders, and persuasions. It is about holding institutions accountable for their policies and practices regarding non-discrimination. In this respect, affirmative action creates competition in the market-place, leading to a greater number of qualified persons competing for every job, with the end results of better value, quality and more productivity, regardless of a worker's race or gender.

There are those like U.S. Representative Newt Gingrich and U.S. Supreme Court Justice Clarence Thomas – to name only two – who seek to narrow this debate to one of race. This serves to alienate women, and lower and middle-strata white males who begin to perceive "unqualified" blacks as their problem. The common theme heard today in the midst of this debate is "They're taking our jobs."

What many persons fail to realize is that to eliminate affirmative action would be to effectively limit access and opportunities for all persons, except those with access to the very top rungs of what remains a rich white-male dominated America.

To limit the debate on affirmative action to one about minority set-asides and race is to create artificial divisions between minorities and women, as well as between minorities and lower and middle-strata white males who desire to move up the socio-economic ladder. It appears that these divisive tactics are being played out by many involved in the affirmative action debate in the political and economic arenas.

Despite the presence of affirmative action over the past 25 years, it is evident for anyone who has sought to navigate the employment waters that many subjective factors continue to play a significant role in hiring processes. As the saying goes, "It's not what you know, it's who you know."

As an African-American with an undergraduate degree from a major research university, and several years of graduate and professional education from very reputable institutions, it would be less than truthful for me to say that I have not benefited in many ways from the struggles for civil and equal rights, and from the enforcement of affirmative action in the various academic institutions I've attended, and career opportunities to which I've had access. Nonetheless, I sense that there are many doors that have not been opened to me, and it has not been because of "what" I did not know, but because of "who" I did not know.

We know that practices of nepotism, cronyism and good-ole-boyism have continued in the work place despite affirmative action. These practices would only become magnified and more pervasive if affirmative action were to be repealed.

To assume that it is every employer's best intention to always hire the best-qualified person for every job is to make a dreadfully false assumption. To assume that it is every academic institution's best intention to always admit the most academically gifted student is to also make a dreadfully false assumption. Any student of 19th and 20th century American history can clearly see that many de-facto practices within the job and academic marketplaces have resulted in less than even playing fields for historically marginalized persons like women and minorities.

To repeal affirmative action would, in essence, serve to re-sanction and re-legitimize discrimination – in its various ugly faces of racism, sexism and classism – throughout our society. This was the case with the laws and practices of the Jim Crow era, and seems to be where America is returning.

Thus, I believe it is incumbent upon all Americans to realize that without some measure of an enforceable affirmative action in our society, the vast majority of us, regardless of our skin-color or gender would find ourselves and our future generations to be the eventual losers.

- Chapter 10 -

WHEN VIOLENCE ABOUNDS: OUR CALL TO ACTION AGAINST VIOLENCE

(This essay was first published as an article in the *United Methodist Connection* of the Baltimore-Washington Conference in June 1999. It was also published by the United Methodist News Service.)

The recent acts of violence that have littered our national and local news should heighten our collective conscious and raise our level of concern. The trial and acquittal of four police officers charged in the death of Amadou Diallo is but the latest episode that serves to remind us of the pervasiveness of violence and hatred in our midst. While the issues surrounding Diallo's death – a West African immigrant who was shot 41 times while unarmed in New York – notably point to the problems underlying some zero-tolerance enforcement policies, and rogue police officers involved in acts of brutality, other instances also serve to point to the permeation of violence in our midst.

Whether it is a 6-year-old boy who brings a gun into a Michigan school and kills his first-grade classmate, or two promising high school seniors in Washington, DC who are gunned down after a basketball game, or a Pennsylvania man who fatally shoots three persons because of his alleged anti-white and anti-Jewish views, we find a plethora of evidence pointing to an increasingly violent society.

Violence abounds. Whether it's the death of Taisha Miller, the young African-American woman murdered by police while sitting in her car in California, or James Byrd, an African-American man who was dragged behind a truck to his death by white supremacists in Texas, or Matthew Shepherd - the young college student who - because of his sexual identity - was beaten, hung on a pole and left to die in Wyoming - violence is all around us.

The problem of violence is complex and multi-dimensioned to say the least. The death of Amadou Diallo – and the lack of justice (heretofore) for those who murdered him - points to the prevalence of racism in America. Racism has resulted in a double standard in many policing practices. These practices are the by-products of policies that tout decreasing inner-city crime rates – but often at the expense of the selective interrogation and arrest of innocent persons of color who fit certain profiles – particularly young African-American males.

Several other factors seem to be complicit in the recent wave of violence in America. Widening economic disparities between the rich and the poor contribute to the escalating violence. We observe that a disproportionate number of those who are victims, as well as many of the alleged perpetrators of violent acts are a part of America's under-class.

Additionally, the ongoing right-wing political influence of the America's gun lobby – spearheaded by the National Rifle Association - seems intent on keeping guns in the hands of any person – of any age – who for any reason wants to possess a handgun. Furthermore – violence in the media and in cyber-space serve as breeding grounds for a preponderance of the intolerance and violent acts that are carried out among us.

What is to be the church's response when violence abounds? First it is incumbent upon the United Methodist Church as a community of the faithful to affirm that the problem of violence in American society is the church's problem. The apostle James shared that "faith without works is not faith at all." John Wesley's notion of social holiness – that we are to "reform the nation and spread Scriptural holiness" - helps us to see that the United Methodist Church is to be prophetically and actively engaged in speaking and acting to eradicate the societal ills that plague us.

Secondly, we must affirm that the problem of violence is shared by all of us. As one of the most diverse communities of faith in the United States, we who are United Methodists are challenged to realize that whether in the city or the suburbs, violence - and its underlying forms of hatred - whether racism, homophobia, sexism or any other forms of xenophobia - must be viewed as our collective dilemma. Violence touches all of our lives, our families and our churches.

Therefore, solving the problem of violence in America is our shared responsibility. Each of our churches - and each member of the United Methodist Church - should prayerfully consider ways that we can constructively address the problem of violence among us. Our collective prayers and thoughts should then spawn us into prophetic social action.

Dr. Martin Luther King, Jr. placed the matter of our faith within the context of peace and justice. King said, "True peace is not merely the absence of tension, but it is the presence of justice." As we strive to become a just church and society, may we all seek to be the peacemakers that Christ calls us to be.

-Chapter 11-

BEYOND TOLERATION: CONFRONTING THE POLITICS OF RACE

(This essay was first published as an article in the *United Methodist Connection* of the Baltimore-Washington Conference in January 2001. It was also published by the United Methodist News Service.)

At the dawn of the 20th Century, W.E.B. DuBois boldly and prophetically declared that the problem of the century would be the problem of the color line. Almost 100 years hence, the problem of color continues to be one that plagues both the society and the church in America. America continues to become increasingly diverse. Within the next two to three decades, there is likely to no longer be any majority population in the country.

With this increasing diversity, there is evidence of ongoing racial and cultural division among us. During this past presidential election, 90 percent of African Americans did not vote for president-elect George W. Bush, while he was able to garner a majority of support among the white electorate. More than 80 percent of America's neighborhoods and schools remain segregated. The majority of Christian churches remain segregated. There are ongoing disparities between whites and all other racial-ethnic groups in terms of employment rates, income, wealth, and access to various essential goods in our society.

Sociological methods of addressing the race problem in America have heretofore dealt essentially with how different races and cultures might co-exist. A common debate has been whether our society is to be viewed in racial-ethnic terms as a "salad bowl" or as "vegetable soup." The familiar refrain of Rodney King, the young African-American man who was the subject of police brutality in California in the early 1990's, has become the clarion call of this approach, "Why can't we all just get along?"

The racial dilemma of the 21st century is one that is a bit more complex than "just getting along." Racism is to be viewed as a political problem that must be addressed in political terms. This is not to say that the church's theology – our vision of inclusivity and unity in Christ, and the social conceptualities and nuances of our society cannot speak in some ways to racism in America, but racism is essentially a political problem in whatever forms and shapes and locations that it continues to be manifest.

Politics in America is closely aligned with economics, and is thus essentially focused on the allocation public goods – who gets what – when, where and how much. Political issues at all levels boil down to how resources are distributed and redistributed. In our new millennial society, the seven major sets of public goods that all politics seek to impact are: (1) education, (2) employment, (3) health-care, (4) housing, (5) safety, (6) technology, and (7) transportation.

Therefore, as much as politics is to be viewed in terms of whether one is a member of the Republican or Democratic or Green Party, politics must be viewed in terms of economics, and ultimately race. The distribution and redistribution of resources in ways that improve the quality of life for persons of all racial and ethnic groups must become a realized vision if we as a society are to overcome racism in the 21st Century.

Thus, the issues central to eradicating racism in America in the future will be issues such as how do we provide quality education for all children in every school in every neighborhood? How do we close the gap in terms of unemployment and underemployment among persons of certain racial-ethnic groups? How do we provide affordable and available health-care and housing for every person in every family? How do we make every neighborhood a safe community – a community of shalom – with the elimination of fratricide, homicide, addiction, police brutality, racial profiling, and all other destructive and deadly behavior? How will we as a society make new technologies – e.g. the Internet - available to every person in every school and every home?

For the Christian church, to grapple with the politics of race is to speak to and act upon the theological concern of God's ideal for the well-being – the shalom – of all humanity. God's desire is that we seek to breech, individually and corporately, the divisions among us – so that through the commonalities of our faith and action, we might discover true peace, justice and unity.

- Chapter 12-

COUNTING THE COSTS: REFLECTIONS ON THE CHURCH AND JUST WAR

(This essay was first published as an article in the *United Methodist Connection* of the Baltimore-Washington Conference in April 2003. It was also published by the United Methodist News Service.)

Amidst the military conflict in which the United States now engages with Iraq, it seems appropriate for the church to continue to consider (and reconsider) the matter of the justice of war from both philosophical and theological perspectives. First, however, the matter of defining "justice" has to be addressed. According to the great philosopher Plato, to speak of justice is simply to deal with the matter of persons getting what they deserve. In light of this brief definition of justice, and regarding the war that is with us, the concern becomes one that is first rooted in the matter of whether or not Iraq and/or the United States is getting what is deserved.

In terms of the morality of war, those who have thought, written, and acted on such matters, have historically raised particular questions as to the determinants of when war might be justified. In the fifth century, St. Augustine, the Christian philosopher, was instrumental in the development of seven criteria for determining whether or not a war is "just." First, there must exist a just cause. The war must confront an unquestioned danger. Second, competent authority must exist. The leader committing a nation to war must be acting on behalf of his/her people. Third, there should be right intention. The reasons set forth should be the actual objectives, and retaliation must not be the aim. Fourth, war should be the last resort. All peaceful alternatives must have been exhausted. Fifth, there needs to be the probability of success. Sixth, discrimination requires the immunity of noncombatants from direct attack. And seventh, the good that will be achieved by war cannot be outweighed by the harm that is done.

In light of the general philosophical criteria outlined here, particular concerns exist as to how these can be applied to the current U.S. war with Iraq. Specifically, do the alleged atrocities and potential threat of Saddam Hussein and the current Iraqi "regime" warrant the "shock and awe" of U.S. military forces, and the concomitant bombing of Baghdad and Basra, resulting in the killing and maiming of countless innocent women, men and children? This is not to speak of the annihilation of an untold number of Iraqi office buildings, shopping malls, factories, schools, mosques and homes.

And for those of us who are Christians, it seems that ours are not only philosophical concerns about whether or not this is a just war, but our concerns center on what it means to live as disciples of Jesus Christ in times like these. And the matter of our attitudes and actions in Christ do not stop with asking the popular question, "What would Jesus do?" For it seems to be clear that Jesus did not - and would not - engage in such atrocities as the war in Iraq. The critical question for the church is also "What is Jesus doing in the lives of Christians today, and how does this lead us to respond?"

It is this preacher's sense that Jesus, who lives in us and through us – the one whom we will exclaim and exalt as the "Living Savior" on Easter – remains steadfastly on the side of the poor, the disinherited, the oppressed, and the dispossessed whether these persons reside in America or the Middle East. Whether in Baghdad or in New York City, it is evident that Jesus lives to offer life, and does not desire death for any purposes - whether political or religious - for any part of humanity.

And so in these times of war, may we who are the church - in our faithfulness - seek to model what Jesus has done, is doing and will do in our world. May we continue to pray and witness to God's will for beloved community among all the people of the world.

-Chapter 13-

CHURCH DIVISION: CAUSE AND RESULTS... THE SLAVE QUESTION AND THE CIVIL WAR

(This essay was first delivered as a lecture at the Howard University School of Divinity in Washington, DC in October 1999. It was also published in the *African Heritage Theological Journal* in June 2001.)

Division: An Introduction

Growing up in the United Methodist Church, it always puzzled me, as to why and how there came to be so many Methodist Churches located so close together. St. Paul United Methodist Church in Oxen Hill, Maryland – the church in which I was baptized and confirmed into full membership – was a small church, all of whose members were African-American. Although I had been baptized and was regularly taken to church by my parents and grandparents, the problem of race in the church really didn't dawn upon me until I was eight years old in 1969.

That was the year that St. Paul Church received its first white minister. That was also the year that there began to be, for the first time, discussions and outward overtures from the white Methodist Church around the corner (Oxen Hill) about shared ministries and possible merger. Up to that point (1969), the two churches seemed to have existed in two separate worlds. Although less than a mile apart, in the same denomination, and supposedly serving and worshiping the same God, the churches were in fact essentially invisible to each other.

It was at the point when serious talks of merger and shared ministry began (circa 1970), that the realities of racial division in the church came to the surface for both the white and black communities. Up until 1968, St. Paul had been a part of the Methodist Church's Central Jurisdiction - the all-black sub-structure created within the structure - concocted by a compromise of Methodist factions in 1939 (to be discussed in detail later), while Oxen Hill had been an established and well-regarded member of the Methodist Church. The merger of the Evangelical United Brethren Church with the Methodist Church, and the subsequent elimination of the (all-black) Central Jurisdiction in 1968 offered new hope that local congregations like St. Paul and Oxen Hill, which had up to that point remained segregated, could heal their racial wounds and work toward reconciliation and eventual union.

Despite the hope engendered by these circumstances, the talk of congregational merger brought the often unspoken wounds and pain of the race problem to the fore. Who would be the pastor of the newly merged congregation? Would she or he be black or white? How would the committees of the new church be established? How would power be shared? In what style would the new congregation worship? The talks of merger eventually ceased, and today these two congregations continue to co-exist less than a mile apart from one another.

The experiences of St. Paul and Oxen Hill United Methodist Churches are not unique within the historical context of Methodism and other denominations. Based upon my early personal experiences and observations of Methodism, along with subsequent experiences while serving in pastoral ministry with four African American United Methodist congregations – one in Southern Prince George's County, Maryland, two in rural Middleburg, Virginia, one in suburban Northern Maryland - and now working with the more than 8000 congregations – white, black, brown, and red – that comprise the Northeastern Jurisdiction of the United Methodist Church - I have continued to hear similar stories of the wounds of racism in the church, as – white, black, red, and brown Christians - seem mired in the unease and uncertainty of how to overcome the racial division that has been so endemic to the church's history in America.

A question rooted in a thought previously raised by Dr. Josiah Young of Wesley Theological Seminary in another quite different context remains before the church. Are Christians who are from diverse ethnic backgrounds really sisters and brothers, or are we merely distant cousins? How closely are we related, and are we ever destined to dwell together as siblings in the same house?

Methodism and John Wesley's Thoughts upon Slavery

It is important to note that John Wesley consistently took a stance that opposed the selling and holding of persons as slaves. William B. McClain points out that Wesley's treatise *Thoughts upon Slavery,* published in 1774, has been assessed by many historians as the most far-reaching treatise ever written against slavery.[1] It was widely distributed and reprinted in England and America. In this pamphlet, Wesley reviled "the enslavement of the noble by barbarous and inferior white men." He appealed to rationality and morality in addition to revelation to condemn slavery:

> But, waiving for the present all other consideration, I strike at the root of this complicated villainy. I absolutely deny all slave holding to be consistent with any degree of natural justice, mercy and truth. No circumstances can make it necessary for a man to burst in sunder all the ties of humanity. It can never be necessary for a rational being to sink himself below a brute. A man can be under no necessity of degrading himself into a wolf...[2]

John Wesley practiced what he preached. According to Wesley's *Journal*, he baptized his first black converts on November 29, 1758, and received them into the Methodist movement. One of these converts was a black woman. These new converts, influenced by Wesley's preaching of experiential faith through which persons are brought into a redeeming conscious fellowship with God, were so filled with evangelistic zeal that they went home and witnessed so persuasively what they had experienced, that their owner, Nathanial Gilbert also became converted to the Christian faith. Gilbert was subsequently licensed to preach as a local preacher in the Methodist movement.[3]

Wesley's theological opposition to slavery was based primarily on his doctrine of grace. For Wesley, grace was rooted in the notion that all creatures bore the stamp of their "maker," thus all persons are recipients of God's prevenient grace. Grace is available and real to all.

To Wesley, one of the most critical points regarding the slave question was that he viewed Blacks as human beings. Slavery was in direct conflict with God's laws of mercy and justice toward persons. In light of Wesley's evangelical message of God's universal grace for all human beings, one of the problems was that those who were enslaved were often considered to be less than human, or non-humans. It was not untypical for persons of African descent to be thought to be uncivilized peoples, or even heathens.

The record of the establishment of the Society for the Propagation of the Gospel (in foreign parts) in 1701 points this out. Formed by the Anglican Church, the SPG was one of the first missionary institutions that sought to convert slaves and Native Americans to Christianity. The debate underlying the work of the SPG was not only rooted in whether or not conversion of slaves and native persons was appropriate or necessary. The conclusion as to this particular aspect of propagation had been addressed by British Royalty in 1660 as Charles II encouraged the evangelization and conversion of slaves in America. The debate was more rooted in who (or what) was being converted – whether slaves and native persons were in-fact persons. Noted black historian Carter G. Woodson points out that the Society's perspective on this question is clearly stated in its mission statement: "to do missionary work among the heathen, especially Indians and Negroes."[4]

To counter these contentions, Wesley offered examples of persons throughout Africa, for example in Guinea, who were not brutal and cruel peoples, and certainly not violent and barbaric by nature.

Wesley cited studies conducted by Monsier Allanson for the Royal Academy of Sciences at Paris to make this point. Concerning both the country and the people of Guinea, the study concludes:

"Which way soever I turned my eyes, I beheld a perfect image of pure nature: An agreeable solitude, bounded on every side by a charming landscape; the rural situation of cottages in the midst of trees the ease and quietness of Negroes, reclined under the shade of the spreading foliage, with the simplicity of dress and manners: The whole revived in my mind that idea of our first parents, and I seemed to contemplate the world in its primitive state. They are, generally speaking, very good-natured, sociable, and obliging."[5]

John Wesley also opposed slavery as a means of helping the new nation in its struggle toward economic independence and prosperity. He pointed out that slavery was not justifiable based on the notion that wealth is considered to be the means to the glory of a country, and that wealth should not be supported through holding other persons captive. Again, it was against God's will, and against moral law that persons be used as chattel property – to be brought and sold as a means of production.

The Wesleyan Doctrine of Grace - Slavery and Black Christianity

Grace, as the integral component in Wesley's construct of the Way of Salvation, required that persons live out faith through loving one's neighbors as was commanded by Christ. Returning to Wesley's opposition to slavery, it is important also to note that he felt that even though slavery was legal in certain parts of the world, it was not justifiable in accordance with the laws of God. He pointed out that man's laws pertaining to slavery and the holding of persons in servitude were flawed at the point where they advocated for or allowed slavery.

From the outset, the notion of universal grace seemed particularly attractive to Blacks who had the privilege of receiving this message. Historian Carter G. Woodson aptly called Black's attraction to the proselytizing by Methodists and Baptists as "The Dawn of a New Day" in the religious development of Negroes. Religious sociologist E. Franklin Frazier pointed out that the proselytizing activities on the part of Methodists and Baptists were a phase of the Great Awakening, which began in New England and spread to the West and South. When Methodists and Baptists began their revivals in the South, large numbers of Negroes were immediately attracted to this type of religious worship.[6]

The conversion of Richard Allen offers insight into the power of the message of universal grace. Converted to Methodism in 1777 at the age of seventeen, his experience was typical of many Blacks.

Allen states:

"... I was awakened and brought to see myself, poor,

wretched and undone, and without the mercy of God, must be lost. Shortly after, I obtained mercy through the blood of Christ, and was constrained to exhort my old companions to seek in the Lord. I went rejoicing for several days and was happy in the Lord, in the conversing with many old, experienced Christians. I was brought under doubts, and was tempted to believe I was deceived, and was constrained to seek the Lord afresh. I went with my head bowed down for many days. My sins were a heavy burden. I was tempted to believe there was no mercy for me. I cried to the Lord both night and day. One night I thought hell would be my portion. I cried to (God) who delighteth to hear the prayers of a poor sinner, and all of a sudden my dungeon shook, my chains flew off, and "Glory to God!" I cried. My soul was filled. I cried, "Enough! For me the Savior died!" Now my confidence was strengthened that the Lord, for Christ's sake, had heard my prayers and pardoned all my sins."[7]

It is clear that Allen's attraction to Methodism was rooted in the evangelical hope that it offered. It was an evangelical message rooted in: (1) The Primacy of Scripture; (2) Conversion as a personal normative experience; and (3) Evangelism as essential to conveying the message of God's grace.

The Roots of Church Division: The Cause

In terms of race relations, the Methodist Church was one of the most progressive religious bodies at the end of the eighteenth century. However, although Methodist evangelists preached a gospel that emphasized that God was "no respecter of persons," and large numbers of Blacks responded favorably to this message, attempts to apply the teachings of John Wesley began to run into opposition when these teachings directly confronted the world of slave masters. In an historical account of the foundations of Methodism in America, it is intimated:

In December 1784, the famous Christmas Conference of preachers was held in Baltimore at Lovely Lane Chapel to chart the future course of the movement in America, a gathering that organized the movement as The Methodist Episcopal Church in America. Most of the American preachers attended, probably including two African Americans, Harry Hosier and Richard Allen. The conference took a forceful stand against slavery and made that witness a featured commitment in the new church's Discipline. Regrettably the church steadily retreated from that courageous stand.[8]

The social customs of the newly formed United States had begun to draw particular lines as to the appropriate social, economic and political strata - and location - of persons based upon race. Blacks invariably occupied a societal position that was separate from and subordinate to Whites. Eventually, this social ordering, and its incumbent racial prejudice and discrimination, had become embedded within the structures of the Methodist Church, as well. Joseph Pilmore, one of the first men (along with Richard Boardman) appointed to a Methodist circuit in America (Philadelphia), pointed out this festering problem in a letter to John Wesley:

"As the ground was wet they persuaded me to try to preach within and appointed men to stand at the door to keep all the Negroes out till white persons got in, but the house would not hold them…"[9]

In attempts to adapt to the growing race problem, many churches began to build balconies or other side rooms for blacks. If separate rooms or seating areas were not practical, they arranged separate services.

The experiences of Richard Allen and other blacks at St. George Methodist Episcopal Church in Philadelphia offer a case in point. An itinerant Methodist preacher after gaining his freedom, Richard Allen arrived in Philadelphia in 1786. After beginning to regularly attend and preach at St. George, Allen sensed the need for a separate place of worship for blacks, but was opposed by both Blacks and Whites. He and other black Methodists began to question the hypocrisy among white Methodists who held slaves, and continued racist practices within houses of worship. In reaction to the segregation policies and practices at St. George, Allen and others would eventually be forced, by conscience, to leave and start a separate worshipping community.

Allen states:

"When the colored people began to get numerous in attending the church, they moved us around the wall, and on the Sabbath morning we went to church ... the sexton stood at the door and told us to go to the gallery." As they were making their way to seats, the minister said, "Let us pray." They apparently knelt in the wrong place because one of the trustees had hold of Rev. Absolom Jones, pulling him off his knees, and saying, "You must get up – you must not kneel here." Mr. Jones replied, "Wait until the prayer is over."[10] Allen continued, "And we all went out of the church in one body, and they were no more plagued with us in the church."

In 1816, the African Methodist Episcopal Church, founded in Philadelphia, became the first black denomination in the United States. Richard Allen was elected the first bishop of the AME church, with the first two congregations being founded as the Bethel Churches in Philadelphia and Baltimore.

African Methodist Episcopal Bishop Reverdy Ransom's thoughts speak to the results of the separation of African Methodists from the Methodist Episcopal Church:

"As to the result of this separation from the Methodist Episcopal Church, permit us to remark that it has been really beneficial to the man of color. First, it has thrown us upon our own resources and made us tax our own mental powers both for government and support: For government - viewed in the light of official responsibility – when we were under control of the M.E. Church we were dependent upon them for ministerial instructions. They supplied our pulpits with preachers, deacons and elders, and these in the vast majority of instances were white men. Hence, if the instructions given were of the right kind, the merit was the white man's and his alone; so also, if the manner of instruction was pleasing, the merit was the white man's and his alone. The colored man was a mere hearer." Secondly, "the separation of our church from the M.E. Church ...has been beneficial to the man of color by giving him an independence of character which he could neither hope for nor attain unto, if he had remained as the ecclesiastical vassal of his white brethren…The circumstances have been such as to produce independent thought; this has resulted in independent action; this independent action has resulted in the extension of our ecclesiastical organization over nearly all of the States and also into Canada; this ecclesiastical organization has given us an independent hierarchy, and this independent hierarchy had made us feel and recognize our individuality and our heaven-created (humanity)."[11]

In 1796 Black Methodists in New York would have similar experiences as African Methodists in Philadelphia in 1786. The result would be their separation from John Street Methodist Episcopal Church. Eventually two separate Black Methodist congregations – the Asbury Church and the Zion Church - would be formed in New York that would lead to the eventual founding of the African Methodist Episcopal Zion Church in 1820 with James Varick as the denomination's first bishop. In its eventual formation into a denomination, two questions remained for the AME Zion church. First, should they join the AME Church, which had been formed in Philadelphia, or second, should they return to the predominantly white Methodist Episcopal Church. The leaders of the Zion movement would decide against both of these options, and eventually adopt a separate Book of Discipline (unlike the AME Church which used the Discipline of the Methodist Episcopal Church with minor adaptation).

It is important to note that the AME and AME Zion Churches were established as *Methodist* Churches. The length of time (AME: 1786 to 1816; and AME Zion 1796 to 1820) between the institutional separation of some Black Methodists from the Methodist Episcopal church, to the establishment of the denominations is worth noting. It is apparent that it was is not the immediate inclination of African Methodists to start new Methodist denominations, but due to ongoing racist practices within Methodist Episcopal Churches, separation became necessary in the eyes of many blacks based upon their spiritual, cultural, social and political needs.

William McClain points out that these new Methodist churches did not condemn the doctrines, nor did they repudiate the polity of traditional Methodism. These were adopted by both African Methodist bodies with few changes and these black churches continue to stand as bulwarks against racism.[12]

McClain further points out that there was a consistent pattern of formation of autonomous Black Methodist Christian communities. The steps included: (1) Integration; (2) Segregation – inhouse segregation came quickly; (3) Separate meeting times; (4) Separate meeting places; (5) Autonomous local organization; (6) Independent local churches; and (7) Regional and National Denominations - with examples being the African Methodist Episcopal and African Methodist Episcopal Zion Churches.

Black Baptists and the Move Towards National Autonomy

The struggles for identity among African Christians in America were not confined to the Methodists. In the nineteenth century, black Baptists were also engaged in organizing and moving toward separate, autonomous national structures. Leroy Fitts in his study, *The History of Black Baptists,* suggests that the discrepancy between the ideal and actual of white Baptist tradition and practices led several black Baptists to follow the example of Richard Allen and the African Methodist Episcopal Church to withdraw from white churches to establish independent churches.[13]

Fitts suggests that the struggle for national organization was focused as much on how to unite black Baptists across regional lines, and how to overcome the debate regarding congregational and regional autonomy, as it was based on dealing with the race question and slavery. Still, within the context of racism and slavery within the church and society, the issue remained how best to deal with the great paradox of the accommodation to slavery on the part of white Baptists in North America.[14]

Some of the first recorded black Baptists were in churches in Providence, Rhode Island and Boston, Massachusetts in 1772. From the founding of the first African Baptist congregation at Silver Bluff across the river from Augusta, Georgia in the colony of South Carolina around 1774, black Baptists had experienced some degree of political, social and spiritual autonomy. This autonomy might – at least in part – explain why the first national Black Baptist denomination was not established until 1895. With the union of the Baptist Foreign Mission Convention (1880), the American National Baptist Convention (1886), and the National Baptist Educational Convention (1893), the National Baptist Convention, USA, was founded in 1895 with E.C. Morris of Helena, Arkansas as the first president.[15]

Ongoing Philosophical Debates – The Church, Slavery and Race
It is clear that with the formation of the Methodist Episcopal Church as a denomination at the end of the eighteenth century, slavery was at the forefront of the church's conscience. How could the church reconcile the holding of slaves with the message of universal grace that it so consistently espoused?

By the start of the nineteenth century, the institution of slavery and the Christian religion had managed to co-exist with minor conflict in the minds of many Christians. On one hand, many persons of high standing within the church had found a way to justify the institution of slavery, while condemning the cruel treatment of slaves by masters. One of these persons was the great evangelist George Whitefield, a contemporary of John Wesley, and considered by many to be of equal standing with Wesley in the broader evangelical Christian community.

Another great evangelical preacher, Samuel Davies, who in 1755 had more than 300 slaves under his pastoral care, supported Whitefield. Davies found nothing about slavery that was inconsistent with the Christian religion. "He pointed out that it was a part of the order of "Providence" that some should be masters and others servants. Christianity did not destroy that relationship, but only regulated it."[16]

In 1756, Benjamin Fawsett, a contemporary of Davies, wrote "A Compassionate Address to the Christian Negroes in Virginia" in which he spoke of the "compatibility" of slavery and Christianity. Fawsett said to the slaves:
"If it pleases God to favour you with good and gentle masters, your obedience to them will not only be easy and pleasant, but you ought to bless and praise God for them."

He went on to say:

> "If, on the other hand, your masters are forward and thereby render your obedience the more difficult, do not therefore cease to pray even for such Masters."[17]

On the other side of the argument were persons such as New England puritan judge Samuel Sewell, who in 1700 wrote one of the first anti-slavery documents, *The Selling of Joseph.* Sewell attacked all the prevailing arguments supporting slavery. Citing one example, Sewell attacked the "positive good" theory, which maintained that slavery was good because it provided an excellent opportunity to make Christians of Africans. To that theory, Sewell simply said that "evil must not be done, that good may come of it."[18]

Another supporter of antislavery was John Wolman who, in the period of twenty-five years between 1743 and 1768, led the fight among his fellow Quakers. Often depressed because he felt his appeal was ignored, eventually Wolman was successful in making Quakers the only denomination to rid itself of slavery prior to the Civil War.

At the Methodist Episcopal Conference of 1780 in Baltimore, the northern preachers went out of their way to require preachers who held slaves to free them:

> Does this conference acknowledge that slavery is contrary to the laws of God, man and nature, and hurtful to society, contrary to the dictates of conscience and pure religion, and doing that which we would not others should do to us or ours? Do we pass our disapprobation on all our friends who keep slaves, and advise their freedom?[19]

At the Christmas Conference of 1784, the Methodist Episcopal Church passed its strongest legislation concerning slavery, calling it an "abomination" that must be done away with. That position unified the Methodist position on slavery. However, that position became more diverse and weaker each year after that.[20] In June of 1785, while still maintaining, "we hold in the deepest abhorrence the practice of slavery," Methodists at a Baltimore meeting voted to "suspend the execution of the minutes on slavery until the deliberations of a future conference."

The rule on slavery was not called up at the next conference. The 1785 General Conference also made changes in the *Discipline* that reflected further compromises. The *Discipline* required that emancipation take place in accordance with the laws of the respective state; it called upon ministers to free their slaves "if it is practicable" and "conforming to the laws of the State in which he lies"; and it established that slaveholders who wanted to join a church must be counseled by a minister "upon the subject of slavery." [21]

Now there existed the conditional allowance for the holding of slaves based upon slave laws, and/or whether slavery was thought to be "practicable."

The 1800 General Conference defeated a motion designed to prevent slaveholders from being admitted as members. This Conference defeated a separate motion that would have set an age limit by which all children born in slavery would have to be set free. The "Affectionate Address" was offered to local congregations as a way of placing responsibility for providing leadership and a voice regarding the slave question not upon the denomination, but again, upon local communities.[22]

Eventually antislavery agitation in the official minutes ceased. The ideological justification for this retreat continued to be that "the Church must preach to the slave even if it could not emancipate him."

Division: Denominational Struggle, Schism and the Civil War

The turn of the nineteenth century brought the continuation of compromise on the slave issue. However, many persons within the Methodist Church refused to compromise. One such person was James O'Kelly who warned, "Slavery is a work of the flesh, assisted by the devil; a mystery of iniquity, that works like witchcraft, to darken your understanding, and burden your hearts." O'Kelly went on to say, "If there is such a being in existence as may be called God, who was the author of this tragedy (slavery); it must be one of those gods that ascend from the bottomless pit. Such a god I defy in the name and strength of Jesus, and proclaim eternal war against him!"[23]

In spite of voices such as O'Kelly's, the Methodist Episcopal Church continued to ignore the issue. In 1836, the bishops warned against dragging the issue of slavery into the church. In an Episcopal letter, they said: "the only safe, scriptural, and prudent way for us, both as ministers and people, to take is wholly to refrain from agitating the subject…" One of the signers of the statement was Bishop James O. Andrew. He became the focal point of the controversy that would divide the Methodist Episcopal Church in 1844.[24]

Bishop Andrew became the owner of slaves when his first wife died. To compound matters, his second wife was also a slaveholder. Realizing that opponents of slavery would use this situation, Andrew offered to resign from the office of Bishop.

The issue was larger than Bishop Andrew, however. Persons against slavery felt that for a bishop in the church to be a slaveholder was the same as the church's support of slavery. They urged Bishop Andrew not to resign. Persons for slavery felt that to yield on this point would overthrow the very principle of slavery. The issue was settled when southern delegates met in Louisville, Kentucky, and formed the Methodist Episcopal Church, South in 1845.[25]

From 1836 to 1845, the Methodist Episcopal Church was forced to review and renew its doctrine of (and practice of) grace, and particularly its understanding of sanctification. Rarely did John Wesley or other early Methodists understand sanctification to mean freedom from all sin. Yet, in response to the question of how Christians are to know if they are saved, John Wesley replied, "We know it by the witness and by the fruit of the Spirit … Indeed the witness is not always clear at first; neither is it afterwards always the same."

Division: The Results –
Ongoing Compromise and Dreams Deferred

The Methodist Church offers one of the clearest cases of the church's general failure or inability to speak prophetically in word and action to the matter of slavery. The split of the Methodist Episcopal Church in 1845 would be a precursor to the actions of the nation, which a few years later would be engaged in a Civil War between the North and the South over the very same issue of slavery.

Between 1844 and 1865, many southern Methodists used their missionary trust among the slaves to essentially maintain the status quo. The termination of slavery as a result of the Civil War eliminated the need to maintain blacks within The Methodist Episcopal Church, South. No longer did the church need to preserve slavery as a way of life. At the close of the war, 207,000 Blacks left the ME Church, South. They joined the two African Methodist denominations, and separate churches being organized by the Methodist Episcopal Church (North). Black Methodist membership in the ME South church would eventually dwindle to below 78,000.[26]

The ongoing effort to rid the church of the race problem did not end for the Methodist Episcopal Church, South with its split with the North. In April of 1866, the General Conference of the Methodist Episcopal Church, South voted to provide for the organization of a separate church based on race. The stated purpose of this action was "to save this remnant" of Black Methodists in the ME Church, South:

> When two or more Annual Conferences shall be formed, let our bishops advise and assist them in organizing a separate General Conference jurisdiction for themselves, if they so desire and the bishops deem expedient, in accordance with the doctrine and discipline of our Church, and bearing the same relation to the General Conference as the Annual Conferences bear to each other." [27]

This resolution led to the creation of five black annual conferences. By May 1870, three more black annual conferences had been added. On December 15, 1870, a decision was made to "allow" black Methodists to split off and form another separate Methodist denomination. The conferences met in Jackson, TN and formed the Colored Methodist Episcopal Church (CME).

William McClain asserts that the racism of the Church's past continues to plague the United Methodist Church – the racial tragedy of Methodism's past persists. Compromise in efforts to sweep the problem of race under the church's "rug" was evident again in 1939 with the Plan of Union between the Methodist Episcopal Church, the ME Church, South and the Methodist Protestant

Church.[28]

For Black Methodists, the results of the "Uniting Conference of 1939" in Kansas City meant the establishment of a "denomination within a denomination – a church within a church." The creation of the all-black Central Jurisdiction was yet another effort of the Methodist Church to rid itself of this problem of race. Black Methodists would be allowed yet again to elect their own Bishops and build their own institutions.

Conclusion

It is clear that problems of racism, and the effects of the various compromises on these matters, continue to affect the Church today. The observation of Dr. Benjamin E. May, the late president of Morehouse College remains true today, "Sunday morning (remains) the most segregated hour of the week." As we enter the new millennium, the problems of race and the color line continue to plague the church and our society.

The question for the church and even for the nation is: will the color line and the problem of race dominate the next century? William B. McClain's question remains before us. "How much longer will we allow racial chauvinism and color xenophobia to sap our energy, block our mission, and blunt our witness?"[29]

It is the hope that persons of faith share in Christ, that offers possibilities for renewal and reconciliation that – given the church's past - we might someday realize the eradication of racism in the church, and unity, peace and justice on earth.

- Chapter 14-

REPAIRING THE BREACH: TOWARDS A THEOLOGY OF RACIAL RECONCILIATION AND RENEWAL

(This essay was first presented as a part of a quadrennial report on Renewal and Reconciliation in July 2004 to the Northeastern Jurisdictional Conference of the United Methodist Church in Syracuse, NY.)

The Theological Task: Responses and Routes to Restoration

The theological task with regard to addressing the problem of racism in the church is essentially contextual and contemporary in nature - and relates to the church's ongoing sense of ministry and mission. A critical theological concern is, "What does God say to the church and society today as it regards racism?" Arising out of this foundational question are several ethical and moral concerns:

- What does this suggest to us about ourselves and our relationships with God and with each other?
- What does God reveal to the church today as it regards human worth and dignity, and the relationship between God and humanity?
- And what is God calling Christians to be and do today?"

In light of these and other questions, four particular theological concerns emerge: repentance, reconciliation, renewal and restoration.

A. Repentance

Given the injury experienced by some of its members because of racism, the church is called to engage in acts of repentance. In 2001, retired United Methodist Bishop James Thomas pointed out that repentance and reconciliation are powerful theological forces, which are much too easily uttered without sufficient reflection by the church. However, Bishop Thomas points out, a moment's reflection reminds us that both are radical biblical concepts.[30]

The need for repentance is rooted in the recognition that all persons are a part of the human family, and specific actions should transpire in affirmation of this reality. There must be a comprehension and appropriation of the intrinsic equality of all persons. The apostle Paul stated, "There is neither Jew nor Greek, there is neither bond or free, there is neither male nor female; for you are all one in Christ Jesus." (Galatians 3:28)

That all persons are a part of the human family entails several presumptions about God the creator, and about humans who have been created by God. Christian ethicist, J. Phillip Wogaman suggests that we presume: (1) *The goodness of created existence.* God created humanity (all humans) in goodness and wholeness. God's divine intention for humanity is goodness and wholeness (shalom). (2) *The value of human life.* In each human being there is sacred and infinite worth as a result of humanity's creation in God's image (imago dei). (3) *The unity of the human family.* Humans have not been created to live in a vacuum, but in community with one another. Because of our creation by the same God, we are all interconnected and interrelated. (4) *The equality of all persons in God.* As God created all persons in the image of God, and as there is unity among humans in God, there is also equal value among all human beings. [31]

Henry Mitchell and Nicholas Cooper-Lewter point out that equality is not merely political rhetoric; it involves God's justice expressed impartially.[32] They further state:

Either God regards all persons as intrinsically equal, or (God) is the unjust author of inequity, the very Creator of the oppressions suffered by persons and groups at the bottom of the social and economic system. As easy as it may be to practice inequality, the American dream will not permit it to be approved by the Creator…The founders of this nation attributed their egalitarian dogma to the very mind of God, and so Americans have believed ever since.

This equality is not to be mistaken for uniformity, however. Americans come in different sizes and shapes. They have various levels of giftedness, in a further diversified spectrum of specialties. They represent a fantastic variety of colors and cultures, from every corner of the earth, to say nothing of the profusion of personality patterns. Still, before the law, they are all equal in standing. Few affirmations have more sweeping consequences psychologically and spiritually, as well as legally, and few are so inadequately articulated, especially in America's circle of power. The pluralism of the dream is far better understood today than ever, but the drift toward the tyranny of single-group supremacy and enforced uniformity is always present.[33]

Racism is to be understood in theological, historical, and sociological context as a form of disunity, disintegration and non-community. By its very nature, racism is antithetical to the realization of unity in the church. In light of this, there seems to be an historical concern that the breach in black/white relations needs to be addressed before we can deal faithfully with other social ills and divisions facing the contemporary church.

Bishop James Thomas points out that often the church wants to avoid the pain of what earlier generations thought to be right at the time. And so, there can easily ensue denial, rationalization or shifting of blame. But when liturgical acts of worship are accompanied by great music, Scripture and the powerful movement of the Holy Spirit, the hope of repentance becomes real.[34]

Repentance involves calling to remembrance the church's racial history. This remembering involves calling persons of faith back to God and one another through our shared ritual, communal, and sacramental life. It also involves telling the history and giving a truthful and accurate account of what has actually occurred. Within the context of our repentance and truth-telling about the church's history, there needs be careful consideration given to the loss of dignity experienced among some persons in the church, as well an accounting of the loss of decision-making power and property that has occurred.

B. Reconciliation

The Christian Church is the body that continuously carries forth the ministry of Jesus Christ in the world. Through its various means of serving the world, the church is the bridge between God and all humanity. It is God working in and through persons, as God continues to reconcile the world unto Godself. "For God was in Christ, reconciling the world unto Godself." (2 Corinthians 5:17-18)

Christ came to break down the barriers that separate persons, and to reconcile persons across our differences. The apostle Paul explicated the role of Christ in uniting and reconciling persons in the church and society:

> Christ is our peace; in his flesh he has made all groups into one and has broken down the dividing wall, that is, the hostility between us... and reconciles groups to God in one body through the cross. So then you are no longer strangers and aliens, but you are citizens with the saints and also members of the household of God, built upon the foundation of the apostles and prophets, with Christ Jesus himself as the cornerstone. In him the whole structure is joined together and grows into a holy temple in the Lord; in whom you also are built together spiritually into the dwelling place for God. (Ephesians 2:14-22)

There is the perception among some in the church that there has not been an appropriate honoring/acknowledgment that Blacks brought a great deal to the 1968 merger that effectively created the United Methodist Church. Thus, there is the need to address the issues of the sense of lost history, dignity, decision-making, and property. The need for reconciliation is based, at least in part, on these and other experiences of injury and loss. The biblical-theological concern with regard to reconciliation is rooted in a question raised by the prophet Ezekiel in the 6th century B.C.E. "Who will stand in the breach? I looked for anyone among them who would repair the wall and stand in the breach...but I found no one." (Ezekiel 22:30)

Reconciliation is closely related to the Hebrew concept *shalom*. Biblical theologian Walter Brueggemann shares that the central vision of world history in the Bible is that all of creation is one, every creature in community with every other, living in harmony and security toward the joy and well-being of every other creature.[35]   Brueggemann continues by pointing out that the Hebrew concept s*halom* – embodied in the notions of reconciliation, peace, salvation and wholeness – is the substance of the biblical vision of one community embracing all creation. Shalom refers to all those resources and factors that make communal harmony joyous and effective. Shalom, as the embodiment of reconciliation, then is to be understood as a synthesis of often changing and conflicting interests. Often what has existed among persons is not an absolute synthesis, but a balance, a compromise and harmony of conflicting interests and agendas that is workable and agreeable to the parties concerned. Each side is generally satisfied with the approach of the other not to resort to means that would drastically alter the existing arrangement.

Even though there is a modicum of tranquility, or at least a temporary balance that is somewhat comfortable for the time being, there continues to be a need to "seek" the peace of every day balance, and "pursue" a higher degree of harmony in the areas that separate humanity. No human being is exactly like another, communities and cultures are distinctive, but the Psalmist's imperative to "seek peace and pursue it" (Psalm 34:14) reminds us that it is God's ideal that persons move toward reconciliation and live together united as one human family.

What then is actually suggested in this exhortation to "Seek peace and pursue it?" To "seek" means to search out opportunities for community. This is consonant and consistent with the first section of verse 14, which states in the imperative form, "Depart (turn away) from evil and do good." In seeking, we "depart" or "turn away from" areas of life that are devoid of shalom, and courageously pursue peace, not permitting apathy or the difficulty of such challenges to hinder or deter us. This interpretation appears satisfactory, but even as we "seek peace" in one area of life, we are commanded and challenged to "pursue" peace in the other realms and at future times.

On a communal level, reconciliation is dependent upon those persons who comprise a particular community. The quest for reconciliation with others is no easy task and frequently requires a balance between individual interests and the broader needs of others. The goal of reconciliation is often elusive. Complete and rewarding personal relationships cannot exist outside "seeking" peace — being sensitized to the needs of others, and then "pursuing" it — addressing and acting upon those impulses with sincere and selfless efforts. But seeking and pursuing reconciliation should not be limited to one occasion, for that will hardly yield a sound and solid relationship. Reconciliation must be perpetually "sought", and deeper relationships than presently exist must be "pursued." In this way harmony between different people with different agendas is realized. We arrive at relationships with others, where we are not necessarily one, but where we dwell together in unity (Psalm 133:1), cognizant always of the realistic balance between being self-concerned and other-concerned.

Christ's concern for reconciliation among persons and various religious and social factions during his time, while not always explicitly stated, was evident in his concern for justice, mercy and love. Justice could not exist without peace, and peace was not possible without justice.

For Jesus, reconciliation did not merely involve a change of beliefs, behaviors and environment, but also a change of heart. This is evident in how Jesus dealt with an invitation to make peace by settling a dispute between two brothers who were quarreling over the division of their inheritance. But he dismissed the request with the pointed question, "Man, who made me a judge or a divider over you?" God's plan of reconciliation is not merely to bring about an outward settlement between (people) *but to create people of goodwill.*[36]

Christ spoke of the vision of reconciliation during the Sermon on the Mount: "Blessed are the peacemakers, for they shall be called children of God." (Matthews 5:9) Every Christian, according to this beatitude, is meant to be a peacemaker both in the church and in the community. It is clear throughout the teachings of Jesus that we should never ourselves seek conflict and be responsible for it. On the contrary, we are called to reconciliation. We are to actively strive for peace with all persons, and so far as it depends on us, we are to live peaceably with all. (Romans 12:18)

Reconciliation is closely related to the love of God as embodied in Christ. "For God so loved the world, that God gave God's only begotten Son, so that whoever believes in Him will not perish, but have everlasting life." (John 3:16)   In Scripture, we are informed, "God is Love." (1 John 4:8) A loving and love-filled God created humanity out of divine love *(agape)*.   It was out of this same love that God sent Jesus into the world.   Unconditional love is the essence of the Greek concept *agape*.   In seeking to create peaceful and just community, God's love must be translated into a love that demonstrates and perpetuates itself through acts of faithfulness toward other persons.   Love within the context of peaceful and just community – when given the choice as to whether (in the words of Miroslav Volf) "to exclude or embrace" the other – will choose perpetually to embrace.[37]

Love, as lived out in peaceful and just community, seeks to embrace other cultures, beliefs, perspectives, and ideologies.   Reconciliation involves developing the capacity to love those who may be considered to be our enemies.   Christ states, "You have heard that it was said that you shall love your neighbor and hate your enemy.   But I say to you, love your enemies and pray for those who persecute you, so that you may be children of your Father in heaven." (Matthew 5:43-45)   Developing the capacity to love one's enemies is a difficult task – and involves perhaps the most radical form of love.

In *Jesus and the Disinherited,* theologian Howard Thurman points to the need for reconciliation in loving one's enemy.   Thurman says:

> To love such an enemy requires reconciliation, the will to re-establish a relationship.   It involves confession of error and seeking to be restored to one's former place.   Doubtless it is this that Jesus had in mind in his charge: "If you bring your gift to the altar, and remember that your brother has sinned against you; leave your gift at the altar... and go be reconciled to your brother and then come and offer your gift." [38]

Martin Luther King, Jr. in *Strength to Love* points out that probably no admonition of Jesus has been more difficult to follow than the command to "love your enemies." With regard to the difficulty found here, King states:

> Some men have sincerely felt its actual practice is not possible. It is easy, they say, to love those who love you, but how can one love those who openly and insidiously seek to defeat you? Others, like Nietzsche, contend that Jesus' exhortation to love one's enemies is testimony to the fact that the Christian ethic is designed for the weak and cowardly, and not for the strong and courageous. Jesus, they say, is an impractical idealist.[39]

As Christians engage in acts of reconciliation and ministries which create peaceful and just community, we essentially endeavor to model the ministry of Christ - a ministry of love, compassion, and reconciliation which sought to address the particular spiritual, social, economic and political concerns of those with whom he came in contact. To engage in acts of reconciliation is to participate in the mission of God, and to live a life in radical service to Christ. As Christ offers peace with justice to the world, the church is likewise called to share in ministries of peace with justice.

C. Renewal

As a vision of hope, renewal is ultimately a call to seek transformation of the communities in which we live. As such, it is a forceful challenge to rise above ourselves – our personal differences — and live according to the plan of God. The Psalmist's exhortation to "seek peace and pursue it" has all the urgency and realism of the law of love and, as such, has the transforming power to take us beyond whatever we thought possible. Paul encouraged Christians in Rome to "Be not conformed to the world, but be transformed by the renewing of your minds." (Romans 12:1) To be transformed, we must first be attuned to our weaknesses.

In seeking renewal, the church is called to reflect upon its actions — past, present and future. The theological imperative of renewal challenges persons in the church to live and act justly, and to participate in processes which will lead to spiritual, social, economic and political transformation of people and their communities.

At the heart of the prophet Amos' vision and challenge to "let justice roll down as waters, and righteousness as an ever-flowing stream" (Amos 5:24) is the hope of transformation of persons and communities. There can be no hopeful enterprise of wholistic community if we do not become aware of the social distortions in our midst, and keep watch over our motives and intentions. We must be willing to critique the genuineness of our love. The hope of community demands that we become critically conscious of the interests and motives that guide our actions.

The ultimate objective of renewal is the transformation of persons and institutions. It is therefore not sufficient to simply maintain the present condition, plight or status quo. The objective is to effect positive and progressive change; to help persons experience the life-transforming, all-enveloping presence and love of God which will empower God's people to stretch beyond the comfort zones of human circumstances. The search is for a creative catalyst that will energize humanity's quest to transform and be transformed. As renewal occurs, and wholistic community is appropriated, lives and relationships are transformed to reflect the reality of *shalom* – the wholeness, well-being, and salvation that is the essence of God's plan.

Theologian Dorothee Solle spoke of the relationship of righteousness to renewal and social transformation:

... 'Grace and truth meet each other, righteousness and peace kiss each other.' (Psalm 85:10) The goal is the state in which God has destroyed the chariots and put an end to aggression. Without social justice, without righteousness, there is no peace. According to the prophets the criterion is the rights of those without rights – for example women and orphans, who have no male advocate. The lowest class is made the criterion for the prosperity of all: those who have been most deprived of their rights, who have the least to say, who not only have no money but also no advocate, no connections, who cannot even go to the authorities because they do not know what they can claim – they are the criterion for what righteousness really is.[40]

As the church engages in processes that promote renewal

of God's people, it endeavors also to model the ministry of Christ — a ministry that was radical, prophetic, visionary, and wholistic in perspective. In engaging in vital ministry that promotes renewal, the church again participates in the mission of God to transform the world.

D. Restoration

The model of ministry as offered to the world by Christ is one of inclusive, universal service. Christ's ministry was directed particularly toward the marginalized: those persons with needs that various societal institutions had failed to address. By feeding the hungry, clothing the naked, and healing those who suffered, Christ demonstrated that the commonality of human strengths and weaknesses far transcends the many forms of diversity that tend to divide persons.

Theologically, restoration is a means of validating repentance and reconciliation, and appropriating the vision of renewal. Restoration ultimately calls Christian churches to do the right thing. Is there a way for the church to equitably share power and resources? What will repentance, reconciliation, and renewal across racial/ethnic/color lines look like, given the cultural and theological differences that are among us? How will wholeness and healing occur amidst the various perspectives that have emerged with regard to restoring relationships in the church, and given the call of many for reparations? Is it possible for Christians to engage in ritual acts of repentance and reconciliation without simultaneously developing means of renewal and restoration?

Restoration will result in systemic change, and will continually enable and catalyze individual transformation. The biblical example of Zaccheus (Luke 19) points to the need for those who have engaged in sinful and unjust practices, which result in the injury of others, to engage in processes that promote systemic transformation and restoration of persons, churches and communities.

Restorative justice based on the Zaccheus model acknowledges that there is a need to repay that which has been unjustly taken. Thus, critical concerns relate to how the church moves forward in mission and ministry, and facilitates the restoration of that which some of its members have lost. How are we to deal with matters of the loss of dignity and decision-making power? How do we address the matter of unjust economics?

In repairing the breach, constructive approaches to restoration could result in developing strategic, wholistic approaches to refurbishing older decaying church buildings inherited by black congregations as many whites who formerly worshipped in urban churches now reside and worship in the relative comfort and safety of suburban communities. The church might develop approaches and commit adequate resources aimed at the wholistic education of the young, and the spiritual, emotional and physical care and empowerment of the dispossessed and distressed. In repairing the breach, the Christian church might create effective models of economic and community development, leading to the creation of jobs that pay living wages, the construction of affordable homes, and the building of state-of-the-art schools.

Ultimately, restoration will be seen in the realization of true authentic community where the church becomes God's instrument of peace, justice and unity on earth.

-Chapter 15-

THE PUBLIC CHURCH AS CULTURALLY INCLUSIVE COMMUNITY

(This essay was first delivered as a lecture at Boston University School of Theology in the Spring of 2000 as a part of The Church in the Contemporary World Project.)

The opportunities for the church and society to become all that God calls us to be lie in our abilities to understand and ultimately value our cultural diversity. Such diversity is found in the various ways that persons differ from one another-and is manifest in forms and distinctions such as race, ethnicity, class, gender, and even age. Our inability-both as a society and as individuals - to deal wholistically and effectively with cultural diversity is evident in the various barriers that we construct to separate ourselves physically, psychologically, and socially.

The reality is that America and the world are rapidly changing. No longer can we simply view ourselves in terms of black and white. Lewis Brown Griggs and Lente-Louise Louw, editors of the series of works, *Valuing Diversity: New Tools for a New Reality*, suggest that differences in culture, ethnicity, gender, race, perspectives, personality, style, values, and feelings need to be honored and encouraged, not merely tolerated. The real value of diversity is that it produces synergistic interactions across difference. It is this synergy that produces unpredictable consequences in terms of breakthrough and results.[41]

In coming to understand diversity, we must develop the capacity to understand ourselves, our own personality in terms of the other. What does our monoculturalism, as termed by Eric Law, the author of *The Wolf Shall Dwell with the Lamb*, have to teach us about what we are to become as a multi-cultural society?

Law suggests that monocultural communities within the context of a multicultural environment, especially for communities of color, are where people can function naturally and comfortably within their cultural boundaries. The purpose of monocultural community is twofold: (1) to find identity and self-esteem as a group; and (2) to do homework together before encountering other cultural communities.

This type of monocultural experience leads to the second type of community where these different monocultural communities can encounter each other in dialogue-thus moving toward a healthy sense of multiculturalism.

Where must we go as a multicultural church and society moving rapidly into post modernity?

Author Bill Easum offers the metaphor of the "Dinosaur" to portray the church in its relationship with society and the popular culture. Easum suggests that in many instances, we are "Dancing with Dinosaurs" while seeking to hold on to many of the vestiges, mores, practices, and traditions of our past.[42]

Perhaps it is the case that for the church to authentically and effectively engage the post modern society in the future, it will have to move beyond this inclination to "Dance with Dinosaurs" and look for innovative and creative approaches for people to relate and interrelate across cultures.

Why is this so important? Easum points out that one of the critical shifts in America will involve the changing nature of the racial-ethnic composition of the country. By the year 2001, one in four people in America will be nonwhite, making the emerging society the most diverse ever.

Easum further suggests that today, the culturally disadvantaged are those white young people raised in the suburbs who are able to converse in only one language. White, Anglo-Saxon Protestants will no longer dominate the emerging world. White-skinned North Americans will experience the same kind of negative treatment they gave to those of different colored skin. Interracial marriages will produce many of North American babies born in the emerging world.

So the critical question seems to be, "How do we creatively deal with the 'Dinosaur' of racial-ethnic exclusiveness?" And, in the midst of such rapid, real, and dynamic change, how do we move toward some coherency as to what it means to be the multicultural, multi-colored, multi-dimensioned people God calls us to be?

In addressing this important question, perhaps it is most helpful to engage in biblical reflection on what it has meant, and what it may mean today and tomorrow to be a part of a multi-cultural community.

We can imagine the days in which Christ lived... the communities in which he was nurtured and subsequently ministered, as being communities of multiculturalism. We can imagine Nazareth, the place where Christ grew to maturity, as a place similar in many ways to many of our diverse communities of today. We recall, the stigma surrounding Nazareth, amidst cultural diversity, as conveyed in the question posited in John 1:46, "Can anything good come out of Nazareth?"

We recall that those in the early Christian community sought to make sense of their multiculturalism. It has been suggested that the community of faith as it gathered on the day of Pentecost essentially comprised the first authentically multicultural congregation. As they gathered for worship on that day, we recall that they were led to speak in several tongues-their native languages- among themselves.

We can imagine that they came as a diverse people-from many nations-and it was in this diversity that God's Spirit helped them to discover the common bond that they shared in Christ.

As the church at Pentecost began to form a multicultural identity, it was their worship in the temple, their following the apostle's teaching, their breaking bread together in fellowship, their ministry with those in need, and their evangelism with those both like and unlike themselves that served to build the faith community that would become the church.

What do we learn from the experiences of the early Christian community? We discover that multicultural community is indeed possible, and certainly necessary to strengthening the church as the community of faith. We learn that within the context of being the church, we have the very essence, the very nature of what it means to be multicultural. We discover that as we - like the early Christians worship together, learn together, break bread together, serve together, and share our faith, we can realize the commonalities that we share in our baptism in Christ.

A study of the early church helps us to see that Christ and his ministry modeled what it meant for the church to be universal in its perspective (globality), catholic in its spirit, yet inclusive in its practice of community-building. This is what the apostle Paul affirmed when he said to the Galatian church:

"In Christ Jesus, there is no longer Jew or Gentile, there is no longer slave or free, there is no longer male or female, for all of you are one in Christ Jesus."   (Gal. 3:28)

To place our human connectedness - our unity, our oneness, and even our globality and diversity – into philosophical terms, I believe that the African construct of Ubuntu is helpful. Ubuntu simply means " the quality of being human." Ubuntu manifests itself through various human acts, clearly visible in social, political, and economic situations as well as among family.

According to sociolinguist Buntu Mfentana, it "runs through the veins of Africans." Lente-Louise Louw in *Valuing Diversity* elaborates on Ubuntu, and states that the quality of being human for Africans is embodied in the oft-repeated proverb, "A person is a person through other people."[43]

Louw goes on to state:

While this African proverb reveals a world view – a metaphysics – that we owe our self-hood to others, that we are first and foremost social beings, that if you will, "no man is a island," or as the African might state, "One finger cannot pick up a grain" – Ubuntu is at the same time, a deeply personal philosophy that calls us to mirror our humanity for each other.

To the observer, Ubuntu can be seen and felt in the spirit of willing participation, unquestioning cooperation, warmth, openness, and personal dignity demonstrated by the indigenous black population. From the cradle, every black child inculcates these qualities so that by the time adulthood is reached, the Ubuntu philosophy has become a way of being.[44]

To emphasize the criticality of Ubuntu, a quote from Anglican Archbishop Desmond Tutu is helpful, "You might have much of the world's riches, and might have a portion of authority, but if you have no Ubuntu, you do not amount to much."

How might we go about developing and fostering multicultural community among ourselves? The following are some of the principles critical to the development of multicultural community:

1.   Invitation. To a great extent, developing multicultural community involves a willingness to accept the invitation ourselves, as well as inviting those who are different from us into cross-cultural dialogue and relationship. Closely related to invitation are the principles of sincerity and intentionality. Raleigh Washington and Glen Kehrein, in their book *Breaking Down Walls: A Model for Reconciliation in an Age of Racial Strife,"* share the importance of sincerity in seeking to relate multiculturally. Sincerity is the willingness to be vulnerable, including self-disclosure of feelings, attitudes, differences, and perceptions with the goal of resolution and building trust. Additionally, they share that intentionality is the purposeful, positive, and planned activity that facilitates reconciliation.[45]

2.   Imagination. Imagination leads us to dream and envision the possibilities for multicultural relationships as the people of God. It is recorded in Scripture that "Where there is no vision, the people perish." (Proverbs 29:1) And it was recorded in Joel's eschatological vision that God declared, "In the last day, I will pour out my spirit upon all flesh, and your sons and daughters shall prophecy, and the old shall dream dreams, and the young shall see visions. (Joel 2:28)

3.   Innovation. Innovation helps us to draw upon the creative gifts that we have been given by God to develop multicultural relationships. What innovative and creative approaches might we take and might our churches and community groups develop, to build multicultural community? What gifts has God given us (music, dance, poetry, capacity-building, consensus-building, other experiences) that might make us more effective in fostering multicultural re-

lationships?

4.   Interaction. Washington and Kehrein refer to a closely
related construct, "interdependence." Interdependence rec-
ognizes our differences, but realizes that we each offer something that other persons need, resulting in equality in relationships. Change strategist Stephen Covey, points out that
interdependence is a higher value than independence. Interaction might begin with dialogue, but it moves us toward
action that is based on the personal strengths that we bring
to the multicultural relationship. In what profound ways
are we being challenged to interact with persons who are
culturally difference from ourselves?

5.   Imperative. Washington and Kehrein refer to this as
call. [46] What does God call us to become as multicultural
community? A sense of divine call has the purpose of leading us into reflection and action that is beyond our human
initiative, desires, and comfort zone.

        Finally, where do we go from here? How do we live out
our identity as God's multicultural people? My mind continues to
return to the image of life being likened to a beautiful mosaic. As
the artist constructs the mosaic, she works on it bit by bit…. slowly,
arduously, meticulously placing every detail of what has been envi-
sioned in her mind into the artistic form that she is creating. The
artist designs the mosaic – constantly striving toward the perfection
of that which began as a vision.

        Life is God's mosaic. It is a mosaic, began at creation, and
yet remaining unfinished. God, the divine artist seeks to make us
into the multicultural, multi-dimensional people that we are called
to become.

        God's vision with this mosaic is that life is "shalom." Bib-
lical theologian Walter Brueggamann speaks of shalom as the substance – the very essence – of the biblical vision of one community
embracing all creation. Shalom encompasses all those resources
and factors which make communal harmony joyous and effective.

        Shalom is a vision of harmony – a vision of covenant community in which we all come to understand Dr. Martin Luther King's notion that "true peace is not merely the absence of tension, true peace is the presence of justice."

Shalom is a vision where we begin to comprehend the great philosopher/theologian Dr. Howard Thurman's belief that true community is the closest manifestation of salvation. In shalom we understand that Christian salvation is ultimately a movement toward authentic community.

Shalom is God's vision for the mosaic that is our world. It is a vision where we come to understand that the God of unconditional grace and redemptive love calls us to perpetually move beyond ourselves, and persistently seek common ground. God calls us to shalom. God calls us to community.

NOTES FOR SECTION TWO

[1] William B. McClain, *Black People in the Methodist Church: Whither Thou Goest* (Nashville: Abingdon, 1984), 12.

[2] John Wesley, *Thoughts Upon Slavery,* quoted by William B. McClain in *Black People in the Methodist Church* (Nashville: Abingdon, 1984), 12.

[3] McClain, 7.

[4] Carter G. Woodson, *The History of the Negro Church* (Washington, DC: Associated Publishers, 1921), 5.

[5] John Wesley, *Thoughts Upon Slavery* (1774), recorded by Albert Outler in *John Wesley* (New York: Oxford University Press, 1964), 85-86n.

[6] E. Franklin Frazier, *The Negro Church in America* (New York: Schocken Books, 1963), 15.

[7] Daniel A. Payne, *History of the African Methodist Episcopal Church* (Nashville: Publishing House of the A.M.E. Sunday School Union, 1891), 72.

[8] *The Book of Discipline of the United Methodist Church* Nashville, TN: The United Methodist Publishing House, 2004), 11.

[9] Related in Joseph Pilmore, *Journal* (Philadelphia, 1769, ed. 1969), 135f.

[10] Richard Allen, *The Life Experiences and Gospel Labors of the Rt. Rev. Richard Allen* (Nashville: Abingdon Press, 1960), 24-25.

[11] Peter Paris, *The Social Teaching of the Black Churches* (Philadelphia: Fortress Press, 1988), 27.

[12] McClain, 8.

[13] Leroy Fitts, *A History of Black Baptists* (Nashville: Broadman Press, 1985), 14.

[14] Ibid., 43.

[15] Ibid., 44-106. Fitts chronicles the history of the founding of the first National Baptist denomination.

[16] Lewis Baldwin and Horace Wallace, *Touched By Grace: Black Methodism in the United Methodist Church* (Nashville: Graded Press, 1986), 32.

[17] Ibid.

[18] Ibid., 33.

[19] Ibid.

[20] Ibid.

[21] Ibid.

[22] Ibid., 34.

[23] Ibid.

[24] Ibid.

[25] Ibid.

[26] Ibid., 39.

[27] Ibid.

[28] William B. McClain, "When a Dream is Deferred: The Racial Tragedy of Methodism, *The Circuit Rider* (Nashville: UM Publishing, March/April 1999), 25.

[29] Ibid., 26.

[30] James S. Thomas, "Repentance and Reconciliation are Radical Actions" by the United Methodist News Service, January 2001.

[31] J. Phillip Wogaman, *Christian Moral Judgment.* (Louisville: Westminster John Knox Press, 1985), see pp. 89-115.

[32] Nicholas Cooper-Lewter and Henry Mitchell, *Soul Theology: The Heart of American Black Culture* (Nashville: Abingdon Press, 1986), 95-96.

[33] Ibid.

[34] Thomas.

[35] Walter Brueggemann, *Living Toward a Vision* (New York: United Press, 1976), 15.

[36] Clarence Jordan, *Sermon on the Mount* (Valley Forge, PA: Judson Press, 1952), 20.

[37] Miroslav Volf, *Exclusion and Embrace: A Theological Exploration of Identity, Otherness and Reconciliation* (Nashville: Abingdon, 1996) Here Volf offers a comprehen-

sive socio-theological exposition of the choice between "exclusion" and "embrace" in intercultural relations.

[38] Howard Thurman, *Jesus and the Disinherited* (Richmond, IN: Friends United press, 1969), 92.

[39] Martin Luther King, Jr. *Strength to Love* (New York: Harper and Row, 1967), 41.

[40] Dorothee Solle, *Thinking About God: An Introduction to Theology* (Minneapolis: Fortress Press, 1975), 156.

[41] Lewis Brown Griggs and Lente-Louise Louw, *Valuing Diversity: New Tools for a New Reality.* (New York: McGraw Hill, 1995), 159.

[42] Bill Easum, *Dancing with Dinosaurs* (Nashville: Abingdon, 1996), Throughout the book Easum develops the metaphor of the church's current state as one of dancing with dinosaurs.

[43] Griggs and Louw, 159.

[44] Ibid.

[45] Glen Kehrein and Raleigh Washington, *Breaking Down Walls: A Model for Reconciliation in an Age of Racial Strife* (Chicago: Moody, 1993). Kehrein and Washington offer an in-depth analysis of *Intentionality and Sincerity* as two important practices in facilitating racial reconciliation.

[46] Ibid.

SECTION THREE

-Chapter 16 -

A PRAYER FOR THE CITY OF BALTIMORE

(This prayer was offered at the Baltimore City Council Meeting on June 14, 2004)

Gracious, all-loving and all-wise God,
 in the busyness of this day, we pause to offer thanks to you.
We come from various directions and locations;
 we come with divergent perspectives;
 we come with a diversity of hopes and dreams and visions.
But we come acknowledging that we gather
 in the commonality that all persons share in you,
 the creator of the universe.
O God, we offer you thanks for the city of Baltimore.
We pray that in the days ahead,
 you'd bless every home and every community of Baltimore.
Bless every school and every place
 where your people gather for work or leisure.
 Bless those persons who are older and those who are younger.
We pray for peace and safety
 for all of us who live and move throughout this city,
 and we pray likewise for communities like ours
 across our nation and world.
We pray that you will bless each of us gathered here.
Most importantly, we ask your blessings
 upon those who serve and lead the city of Baltimore
 in elective or appointive office.
Bless them with a portion of wisdom, patience,
 integrity, justice and compassion.
Bless each of those who serve and lead

that they will be forever mindful of a collective commitment
to act in ways that facilitate the betterment
of each person, each home, each school, each community,
and each place of business of Baltimore.
Be with each of us now and forever, we pray. Amen.

-Chapter 17 -

HOWARD THURMAN
AND THE IDENTITY OF JESUS

(This essay was originally presented at the Center of Theological Inquiry, Princeton University in June 2004.)

Howard Thurman is considered by many to have been one of the seminal American religious figures of the 20th century. Recognized in 1953 by *Life Magazine* as one of the twelve greatest preachers in America, Thurman was variously described as a pastor, theologian, philosopher, mystic and prophet. Throughout his ministry, he sought to draw upon the raw materials of life as a critical resource of Christian faith in ways that would address his overarching theological concern for the articulation and appropriation of a Christian witness that would give impetus to personal spiritual growth, while ultimately actualizing social transformation and authentic community.

This essay will examine Howard Thurman's Christology in light of this concern. It is proposed that his Christology - and the explication of the identity of Jesus of Nazareth in his work - was foundational to Thurman's overall theological project, and ultimately served as the framework for his conception of the ministry and mission of the Christian church.

The grandson of slaves, Howard Thurman came out of the black religious tradition with a message of hope and wholeness for all people. Born in segregated Daytona, Florida on November 18, 1900, Thurman stayed in that city until the absence of educational opportunities for Negroes forced him to go to Jacksonville, Florida for a high school education. He completed undergraduate studies at Morehouse College in Atlanta, Georgia in 1923 and graduate theological studies at Rochester Divinity School in Rochester, New York in 1926.

Thurman's ministerial career formally began in Oberlin, Ohio where, from 1926 until 1928, he pastored an African-American Baptist congregation. From 1932-44, he served as Dean of Rankin

Memorial Chapel and Professor of Theology at Howard University. In 1953, Thurman became the first African-American dean at a majority white university, the Dean of Marsh Chapel and Professor of Spiritual Resources and Disciplines at Boston University. During this same period, he formed the Howard Thurman Educational Trust, which disburses funds for various humanitarian endeavors, most notably scholarships for African-American students in the South. Prominent among his many involvements, however, was the San Francisco based church which he co-founded and co-pastored from 1944-53 – The Church for the Fellowship of All Peoples (Fellowship Church) – heralded as the first authentically inclusive model of institutional religion in the United States.[1]

Howard Thurman was a multidimensional person who lived on all levels of existence – physical, emotional, and spiritual. Describing his attributes is like constructing a bridge. The bridge, to be effective, must reach both sides, or the traveler will fall.[2] Vincent Harding captured the essence of Thurman as a "God-intoxicated" man when he wrote about Thurman in the introduction to *For the Inward Journey*. Harding observed that Howard Thurman was a person who was constantly moving toward the source of all human life and truth via the concrete beauty and terror of the black experience in the United States.[3]

Lerone Bennett, Jr. in his eulogy of Thurman in 1981, pointed to Thurman's perspective on life, "A man cannot be at home everywhere, unless he is at home somewhere."[4] One has to know from whence he has come in order to understand how he is to operate within the context of present reality and future possibility. Thurman seemed to be at home with his roots in Southern black culture, and yet was able to practice ministry in ways that crossed cultural and theological perspectives.

His search for community was intricately connected to the yearning for an irreducible essence as rooted in his own search for a Christ-centered spirituality and sense of connectedness with God. This yearning for God-connectedness is evident in Thurman's prayer:
Lord, I want to be more holy in my heart.
Here is the citadel of all my desiring,
where my hopes are born,
and all the deep resolutions of my spirit take wings.

In this center, my fears are nourished,
and all my hates are nurtured.
Here my loves are cherished,
all the deep hungers of my spirit are honored
without quivering and without shock.
In my heart, above all else,
let love and integrity envelop me
until my love is perfected and the last vestige
of my desiring is no longer in conflict with thy Spirit.
Lord, I want to be more holy in my heart.[5]

Thurman's desire to experience God is further articulated in another prayer:

O Holy God,
open to me
light for my darkness,
courage for my fear,
hope for my despair.
O loving God,
open for me
wisdom for my confusion,
forgiveness for my sins,
love for my hate.
O God of peace,
open for me
peace for my turmoil,
joy for my sorrow,
strength for my weakness.
O generous God,
open my heart
to receive all your gifts.

In his work, Howard Thurman sought to "utilize the raw materials of daily experience as the time and place for the encounter with God."[6] He viewed nature as critical to helping persons understand the life of the spirit. At one point he compared life to a river. The river flows constantly seeking to connect with its source

– the sea. In human life, persons perpetually seek to discover that which is the source of life – the source of being and the source of meaning. That being the divine source.[7]

In his reflection, "The Will to Live," Thurman wrote of once walking down a street in Georgia, and observing a tree that had broken through the concrete pavement. The pavement could not contain the tree's desire to live. In spreading itself and breaking through, the tree demonstrated its determination to live. He writes:

> You have seen trees growing out of sheer rock; or roots, finding no soil below or being unable to penetrate the rocky substance of the earth, spread themselves, fan shaped, on the surface, sending their tendrils into every crevice and cranny where hidden moisture and soil fragments accumulate. You have seen human beings with their bodies reduced to mere skeletons and all the vestiges of health wiped out – yet for interminable periods they continue breathing, as if to breathe were life.[8]

Howard Thurman's yearning for the fullness of life and for an appropriation of community was rooted in his own spirituality. In *Meditations of the Heart,* he wrote:

> Here is in every person an inward sea, and in that sea there is an island and on that island there is an altar, and standing before that altar is the "angel with the flaming sword." Nothing can get by that angel to be placed upon that altar unless it has the mark of the inner authority. Nothing passes "the angel with the flaming sword" to be placed upon your altar unless it is a part of "the fluid of your consent." This is your crucial link to the Eternal.[9]

Intellectual and Spiritual Influences on Thurman's Christology

George Cross taught Howard Thurman systematic theology during his last year and a half of seminary education at Rochester Divinity School (1925-1926). The influence of Cross on Thurman can be seen first in Cross's pursuit of an element which he could identify as the *essence* of the Christian faith. It is the basic, unchanging, unifying truth that characterizes and genuinely manifests the faith. This essential truth may be found in Christian doctrines, dogmas, creeds, and theologies, but it is never fully contained in them. This essential truth has the fundamental qualities common to all religions, yet it is distinctive within Christianity, according to Cross.[10]

The essence of Christianity is what Cross endeavored to define through his method for doing apologetics.[11] This essence is characterized in the following ways:

1. It is "a quality of spiritual life," where one acknowledges that one's ultimate interests and commitments must be with spiritual concerns.
2. The personality of Jesus Christ is the basis for understanding the essence. In Jesus, the Christian finds the perfect life. And through spiritual fellowship with this perfect life, its teachings and the meaning of its example, the Christian finds the way to "the higher life."
3. It has distinctive qualities that are similar to other religions. It takes the individual into a consciousness of the relation to God, which brings fulfillment to the heart like no other religion. Other religions are "Christianity in its beginning or lower stages."[12]
4. It is the practice of the most perfect fellowship, where the potentialities in every person are appreciated, developed, and made available to the needs of others.
5. It is "one and the same with true morality." Love and devotion to God mean love and devotion to the welfare of our fellow man and woman.
6. It has the power for moral redemption, such that it delivers humanity from the domination of evil.
7. It creates the experience of perfect peace for the believer. In the midst of suffering, fear and anxieties, this essence gives confidence and power to withstand and overcome.

The teleology of George Cross's conception of Christian essence is to lead the individual and community toward salvation. In his book, *Christian Salvation,* Cross defines salvation this way:

...to the modern Protestant it is the bringing of the man into such a fellowship with God as gives him a self-mastery and a self-devotion to the highest end of life. It is the entrance into an experience of conscious unity of life with one's fellowmen, a participation in the ministry of a universal good. It is to be endowed with that spirit of enterprise that enables him to turn the forces of the material world toward their true end, to make them angels of mercy sent forth to do service for the sake of them that shall inherit salvation.[13]

According to Cross, there must be individual salvation before a community can be saved. Christian salvation is ultimately the movement toward "perfect community" or "shalom." Perfect community for Cross is actualized at the place and time where persons are able to exercise their full potential and be in loving relationship with other individuals.

Howard Thurman's major disagreement with the Christian liberalism espoused by George Cross was the extreme positivism it displayed. Its unmitigated belief in national destiny and world progress served to obscure the malignancy and pervasiveness of domestic evils, particularly as regards racism. For Thurman, a theological stance which so readily ignored hostilities directed at large segments of the population (African Americans, women, various immigrant groups, etc.) was seriously impaired. He believed that such optimism was a critical if not fatal departure from social reality, and was utterly irreconcilable with his own experience as one of the dominated and disinherited.

Despite Thurman's attestation that Cross was the teacher who had a "greater influence on my mind than any other person who ever lived," he remained at variance with the idea of leisurely introspection as the means to human attainment. Thurman shared deeply the concern of Cross and Henry Robins (professor of Religious Education and the History and Philosophy of Religion and Missions at Rochester Divinity School while Howard Thurman was a student there) for the centrality of human personality, the universal life of the spirit, and other liberal motifs, but he had to express the "hunger of the spirit" which they encouraged inclusive of his own racial fact.[14]

While scholars like Cross and Robins significantly impacted

Howard Thurman's intellectual development, it was his maternal grandmother, Nancy Ambrose who cultivated his identification with Christ from an early age. Of his grandmother, Thurman says:

> I learned more, for instance, about the genius of the reli-
> gion of Jesus from my grandmother than from all the men
> who taught me all ... the Greek and the rest of it. Because
> she moved inside the experience and lived out of that kind
> of center...[15]

Reared by his beloved Grandma Nancy, a former slave, young Thurman regularly read the Bible aloud to her as a child. Nancy Ambrose was not a scholar *per se,* but a sapient personality who understood the value of a cultivated mind. As a young girl living on a Florida plantation in the antebellum period, no prospects for liberty existed, but early on she established the grounds for freedom. Liberty was conferred from without, but freedom, she discovered, was founded from within. She never received a formal education, yet she was acutely aware of its importance. When the owner's daughter was punished for trying to teach her the rudiments of reading and counting, Nancy Ambrose knew "there must be some magic in knowing how to read and write."[16] Later, she would communicate to her grandson a fundamental reason for obtaining the "magic" of knowledge, sharing this message: "Your only chance is to get an education. The white man will destroy you if you don't."[17]

From her Thurman learned not only of the trials of slavery, but also of the slaves' deep religious faith, which profoundly shaped his vision of the transformative promise of Christianity. Nancy Ambrose appropriated a "religious essence" that was not just in dialogue with concern for the world, but with the particular issue of what it means to be black in America. Howard Thurman was profoundly influenced by the views of his grandmother on religion and racism. Much of her thinking is captured in her views of Scripture. Thurman writes:

> Two or three times a week I read the Bible aloud to her. I
> was deeply impressed by the fact that she was most par-
> ticular about the choice of Scripture. For instance, I might
> read many of the more devotional Psalms, some of Isaiah,

the Gospels again and again, but the Pauline epistles, never – except at long intervals, the thirteenth chapter of First Corinthians... With the feeling of great temerity, I asked her one day why it was that she would not let me read any of the Pauline letters. What she told me I shall never forget. "During the days of slavery," she said, "the master's minister would occasionally hold services for the slaves. Old man McGhee was so mean that he would not let a Negro minister preach to his slaves. Always the white minister used as his text: 'Slaves, be obedient to your master... as unto Christ.' Then he would go on to show how it was God's will that we were slaves and how, if we were good and happy slaves, God would bless us.   I promised my Maker that if I ever learned to read and if freedom ever came, I would not read that part of the Bible."[18]

In contrast, she often told the story of the black preacher who had a different message for the slaves. In their gathering he would say: "You are not slaves, you are not niggers – you are God's children." As his grandmother finished her story with those lines, a kind of transformation took place in her. According to Thurman: "she would unconsciously straighten up, head high and chest out, and a faraway look would come on her face."[19]

Jesus and the Christian Love-Ethic
Howard Thurman's Christology was rooted in his experiences of being personally victimized by racism. He was acutely aware that racism attacked his self-worth and freedom. His mystical experiences, however, provided the assurance that he was a beloved child of God, and that harmonious relatedness is the underlying structure of reality. Racism denied the truth about God's intent for creation. It put the welfare of the community in crisis. The prophetic questions for Thurman became: How could he help shape a social reality that conformed to his religious beliefs? How could he speak to the crisis by restoring the community's (especially America's) sense of well-being.[20]
Jesus of Nazareth, in Howard Thurman's mind, is the revelation of how personality creates community; Jesus personifies the

transforming power of love. The conditions and circumstances of Jesus' life are significant in understanding Christianity and the meaning of Jesus in the world.[21]

Thurman began to outline more fully the basic principles of his philosophy of the Christian love-ethic in the early part of 1935 at the annual convocation on preaching at the School of Theology of Boston University.[22]   In 1948, he delivered a series of lectures at Huston College (now Huston-Tillotson College) in Austin, Texas, and in 1949 published, *Jesus and the Disinherited,* which gave a radical perspective of the mission, ministry and teachings of Jesus, as compared with the general view of the majority culture. Throughout, Thurman showed that Jesus' ministry in the world addressed the needs and aspirations of the disinherited. He pointed out that the concern of Jesus is still for the disinherited.[23]

Historian Lerone Bennett asserts that *Jesus and the Disinherited* offers perhaps the most comprehensive analysis of the Christian love-ethic.[24] Bennett further suggests that Thurman had a great influence on Martin Luther King, Jr. and his thinking on the Christian love-ethic. When Bennett went to Montgomery, Alabama, shortly after the beginning of the Montgomery Bus Boycott, he was not at all surprised to find King reading not Mohandas Gandhi, but Howard Thurman.

Author and activist, Vincent Harding, recalls that Thurman's *Jesus and the Disinherited* was used by leaders in the civil rights movement as a theological foundation for their activism. They would regularly study and discuss the book together. It provided crucial instruction on nonviolence and the love-ethic as Christian means for overcoming social oppression. The leaders could better understand how to define and maintain their religious identity in the midst of political struggles.[25] Harding believes that this text defined the spiritual issues for social transformation, and that it inspired and emboldened leaders as they engaged in the struggle for justice.

In *Jesus and the Disinherited,* Thurman emphasized the social circumstances of this poor and oppressed Jew, and then concluded that the religion of Jesus was a creative response which emerged from and dealt with transforming these conditions of oppression and sought to develop authentic community.

Thurman sought to explicate the ethical insights of the Jewish prophets, as interpreted through the life of Jesus. The ethical example of Jesus continues to have relevance for people who find themselves backed up against the wall. How ought the impoverished ethnic and religious minorities respond to the material and spiritual assaults of imperial oppression? The example of Jesus suggests a response of courage, truth telling, and love. [26]

For Thurman, there was no possibility of community without careful and constructive attention to the *disinherited*. He proclaimed that the mistreatment of America's *disinherited* and acceptance of "the will to segregate" are betrayals of American and Christian ideals of community-building.

Howard Thurman concluded that love is the force that creates full community, and nonviolent change is the best expression of love. He considered the terms "reconciliation" and "love" to be synonymous.[27] He defined love as "the intelligent, kindly but stern expression of kinship of one individual for another, having as its purpose the maintenance and furtherance of life at its highest level."[28] Love responds to an individual's basic need of being cared for. It participates in the attempt to actualize potential, and therefore completes the fragmented and unfulfilled personality. But on a larger scale, it brings together separated lives. It makes apparent the significance of relationships by stressing how inter-dependence is inherent in all of life. Love creates community.[29]

His *Disciplines of the Spirit* (1963) went further to explain the relationship of the Christian love-ethic to the spiritual quest for wholeness.[30] Thurman stated:

Since the will to segregate is a spiritual problem, only a spiritual answer which affirms the binding attributes of love will suffice. Violence is the act through which the nonexistence of the other person is willed, with hate as the dynamic. At the same time this is an act of self-affirmation, for hate becomes a man's way of saying that he is present. Ultimately, the human spirit cannot tolerate this because it denies the elemental truth of life that "men are made for each other." Violence is in opposition to the "fact of the underlying unity of life." Violence is in opposition to full community.[31]

Thurman understood racism to be a contradiction to life

(the teachings of Jesus).[32] Racism is inimical to the formation of identity. Neither blacks nor whites can attain a proper sense of self and give full expression to their potential in an environment of prejudice, segregation, and violence. Racism is also inimical to the formation of community. Systematic discrimination sabotages the function of community as a place of nurture and growth through cooperation. Destructive forces are released to rupture life's inter-relatedness.[33]

He wrote of the need to overcome hatred as a prerequisite for overcoming racism and building community.[34] His construct for understanding hatred begins in a situation where there is *contact without fellowship*. This is contact that is devoid of any of the primary overtures of warmth and fellow-feelings and genuineness. Secondly, Thurman points out that contacts without fellowship tend to express themselves in the kind of *understanding that is strikingly unsympathetic*. There is understanding of a kind, but it is without healing and reinforcement of personality. Thirdly, Thurman points out that unsympathetic understanding tends to express itself in the *active functioning of ill-will*.

To make this point, he shared the story of once traveling from Chicago to Memphis, Tennessee.[35] He found his seat on the train across from an elderly lady, who took immediate cognizance of his presence. When the conductor came along for the tickets, she said to him, pointing in Thurman's direction, "What is *that* doing in this car?"

The conductor answered, with a touch of creative humor, "*That* has a ticket."

For the next fifty miles, this lady talked for five or ten minutes to all who were seated in that coach, setting forth her philosophy of human relationships and the basis of her objection to Thurman's presence in the car. Thurman said that he was able to see the atmosphere of the entire car shift from common indifference to active recognition of and, to some extent positive resentment of his presence in the car. He said, "An ill will spreading is like a contagious virus."

Fourth, Thurman suggests that active ill-will, when dramatized in a human being, becomes *hatred walking on earth*.

Jesus and the Quest for Community

Amidst racism and other forms of hatred, Howard Thurman maintained that the religion of Jesus makes the love-ethic and the quest for community central. Regarding this, he stated:

This is no ordinary achievement. It seems clear that Jesus started out with the simple teaching concerning love embodied in the timeless words of Israel: "Hear, O Israel: The Lord our God is one Lord: and thou shalt love the Lord thy God with all thy heart, and with all thy soul, and with all thy might," and "thy neighbor as thyself." Once the neighbor is defined, then one's moral obligation is clear.[36]

Thurman offered the story of the Good Samaritan as an example of how the love-ethic works:

In a memorable story Jesus defined the neighbor by telling of the Good Samaritan. With sure artistry and great power he depicted what happens when a man responds directly to human need across the barriers of class, race, and condition. Every man is potentially every other man's neighbor. Neighborliness is nonspatial, it is qualitative. A man must love his neighbor directly, clearly, permitting no barriers between.[37]

Thurman spoke of the difficulties faced by Jesus in attempting to teach and live out this love-ethic:

This was not an easy position for Jesus to take within his own community. Opposition to his teaching increased as the days passed. A twofold demand was made upon him at all times: to love those of the household of Israel who became his enemies because they regarded him as a careless perverter of the truths of God; to love those beyond the household of Israel – the Samaritan and even the Roman.[38]

Howard Thurman identified community as the single most important quest of human life. It had occupied his thoughts and activities since childhood. Defining and appropriating community was the end purpose of Thurman's theology, with Christian love being the means – the instrument – for the realization of community. Establishing community was the commitment and labor of his ministry. [39] The basic principle behind Howard Thurman's concept of community was that "the literal fact of the underlying unity of life seems to be established beyond doubt." He developed this principle in saying:

If life has been fashioned out of a fundamental unity and ground, and if it has developed within a structure, then it is not to be wondered at that the interest in and concern for wholeness should be part of the conscious intent of life, more basic than any particular conscious tendency toward fragmentation... It (reconciliation) seeks to effect and further harmonize relations in a totally comprehensive climate.[40]

For Thurman, true community is also the clearest manifestation of salvation. The essence of Christian life is to lead individuals and communities towards wholeness *(shalom)*. Christian wholeness – according to Thurman – is ultimately the movement towards "perfect community."

Thurman's personal encounters with racism would serve to strengthen his resolve for community. He would share:

I know that the experiences of unity in human relations are more compelling than the concepts, the fears, the prejudices, which divide. Despite the tendency to feel my race superior, my nation the greatest nation, my faith the true faith, I must beat down the boundaries of my exclusiveness until my sense of separateness is completely enveloped in a sense of fellowship. There must be free and easy access by all, to all the rich resources accumulated by groups and individuals in years of living and experiencing.[41]

Regarding love of one's enemy, Thurman went on to state:

Love of the enemy means a fundamental attack must first be made on the enemy status. How can this be done? Does it mean ignoring the fact that he belongs to the enemy class? Hardly. For lack of a better term, an "unscrambling" process is required. Obviously a situation has to be set up in which it is possible for primary contacts to be multiplied.

By this I do not mean contacts that are determined by status or by social distinctions. There are always primary contacts between the weak and the strong, the privileged and the underprivileged, but they are generally contacts within zones of agreement, which leave the status of the individual intact. There is a great intimacy between whites and Negroes, but it is usually between servant and served, between employer and employee. Once the status of each is frozen or fixed, contacts are merely truces between enemies – a kind of armistice for purposes of economic security.[42]

Clearly, Howard Thurman's conception of Christian love was rooted in the example of the unconditional love of Christ. The practice of unconditional love is essential to the breaking down of social barriers such as racism. Thurman suggests that nonviolent protests (i.e. boycotts, non-cooperation, demonstrations, sit-ins) are key means of providing shock and transforming the social order. The development of a philosophy of nonviolent protest in the black struggle is a foremost achievement of his social witness. Here, Thurman makes a signal contribution to providing a peaceful method for change in American race relations. Luther Smith argues that Thurman has done more than any other person to articulate the ethical and spiritual necessity for blacks' civil liberties struggle to be grounded in the principles of nonviolence. As early as 1928 in his article, "Peace Tactics and a Racial Minority," Thurman began to outline how a "philosophy of pacifism" can begin to eliminate whites' will to control and blacks' will to hate. His primary concern was to call a truce to attitudes which promote separation.[43]

The loving community of peace, justice and equality can only be attained by loving means. Community cannot be built on the tools of hatred. Nonviolence responds in a caring way to the perpetrator of violence. It announces that the well-being of the individuals involved is of ultimate concern. It moves the level of confrontation to a higher spiritual plane. Instead of merely defeating one's offender physically or psychologically, one begins to create the climate for love to be a force, which has to be dealt with within the context of relationships and fellowship. The presence of loving care introduces new possibilities for reconciliation. Only nonviolence permits love to enter conflict creatively and address the prevailing spiritual ills of separation, fear and hatred.

For Thurman, the formation of community is the teleology of Christian life. The vision of community- as embodied in the life of Jesus - gives value, structure, and purpose to life; it saves life from meaninglessness, frustration, despair, boredom, anxiety, and chaos. Community is salvation; it is life at its highest level.[44] Community (salvation) is not a beyond-this-world hope, but is a possibility for God's love to triumph in history. Jesus' message of salvation is eschatological in the sense that it pronounces the ability to experience salvation here and now.[45]

The essence of evangelical liberalism affirms a religious teleology in which Christianity wins the world to profess Jesus Christ as Lord. The saved community is the Christian community. The Kingdom of God is more precisely the Kingdom of God in Christ. Christianity's goal is to convert individuals and societies to "the way" of Jesus; any achievement less than this is inadequate.[46]

Jesus as the Source of Liberation and Hope

For Howard Thurman, the church has been uniquely and singularly Christocentric. This is particularly the case for the Black churches. Teaching, preaching and living the hope that is in Christ have been key means of survival amidst the oppressive structures and realities historically incumbent for Blacks in American society, and have been foundational to informing the African-American hermeneutic. The emphasis on Christ as the liberator transcends the allegorical and typological approaches to the interpretation of Scripture. This Christocentric focus undergirds the expectation of spiritual, social and political liberation.

This focus is evident in Jesus' sense of mission as embodied in the notion of the "liberation" of humanity. This is made clear in the famous Lukan text:

> The Spirit of the Lord is upon me.
>> because God has anointed me
>> to bring good news to the poor.
> God has sent me to proclaim release
>> to the captives and recovery of sight to the blind.
>
>   (Luke 4:18-19)

In this text Jesus essentially speaks to the universal nature of the hope that is found in his conception of a liberating ministry for all those who were oppressed. Jesus was passionately concerned with the condition of all people, especially the oppressed of the earth. He demonstrated this concern by his association with the despised and disinherited persons and groups of his own time.

It is the cross and resurrection of Christ that gives ultimate expression to these concerns of human liberation. The cross (Christ's crucifixion) provides a unique angle of vision for understanding the multidimensionality and universality of human suffering. The resurrection symbolizes the promise of new possibilities for meaning, life and hope in the midst of and beyond the existential sense of dread and despair. This serves as an alternative to meaninglessness or nihilism.

Here, Thurman's views are similar to those of Dietrich Bonhoeffer. The cross was the end, the death of the Son of God, curse and judgment upon all flesh. If the cross were the last word on Jesus, the world would be lost in death and damnation without hope, and the world would have been victorious over God. But God, who alone effected salvation for us – "all this is from God" (2 Cor. 5:18) – raised Christ from the dead. That was the new beginning following the end as a miracle from above, though not like the springtime according to a fixed natural law, but rather according to the incomparable freedom and power of God that shatters death.[47]

Thurman could attest to the critical nature of the life of Jesus as a foundation for comprehending and appropriating Christian hope. The message of hope was one that believers in the early church would preach as the cornerstone of the Christian faith. The message of hope - ultimately embodied in the resurrection of Christ - underscores the nature of Jesus, who in the minds of many followers had entered into salvation history as the embodiment and fulfillment of the messianic promise. The message of hope was one that black slaves in America would sing, preach and pray as means of communal and existential survival.[48]

For Thurman, resurrection hope from a Christian perspective differs from that of mythology insofar as it directs us to the life here on earth in a completely new and, compared to the Old Testament, more incisive fashion. Christians must partake of earthly life to the very end, just as did Christ ("My God, my God, why have

you forsaken me?" (Matt. 27:46)), and only by doing so is the Crucified and Resurrected with them, and are they themselves crucified
and resurrected with Christ.

Thurman further suggested that Christian faith does not
overstep these realities into a heavenly utopia, but seeks to address
these realities within the context of what he referred to as the "raw
materials" of faith and life. It is in following Christ who was raised
from suffering, from god-forsaken death and from the grave, that
we gain an open prospect in which there is nothing more to oppress
us, a view of the realm of freedom and of transformation. The gospel message of Christ calls for personal, communal and systemic
transformation.

Christian faith does not flee the world, but lives with hope
into the future. To believe in Christ, in fact means perpetually seeking to transcend bounds, to be engaged in an ongoing journey towards transformation. Yet this happens in ways that do not seek to
suppress or avoid the unpleasant realities of the world. Death and
suffering are real.

In Christ, there is evidence of God's breaking into history
to transform suffering into wholeness - to move persons from victims to liberated change agents. In Christ, God has spoken against
evil and injustice. In Christ, the oppressed are set free to struggle
against injustice, and humanity is liberated to move beyond suffering and oppression, and towards an appropriation of hope and life.
The cross and empty tomb are evidence of the reality that "death
has been swallowed up in victory" (1 Cor. 15:54); that hope over-
comes despair; that peace with justice is possible amidst injustice;
and that liberation and transformation may be realized amidst oppression. The cross and resurrection are evidence that life is ultimately possible amidst impending death.

Concluding Thoughts: Thurman, Jesus and the Church Today

Any notion of applying Thurman's Christological thought
and praxis to the church's life today begins at the point of considering who Jesus was/is as the embodiment of the disinherited. Regarding the identity of Jesus, Thurman points out that:

Jesus was poor. He was not a Roman citizen like Paul and
was therefore outside the circle of real privilege. He was a
carpenter. He did not write a book. He did not travel very

far from his home. He was tender without being soft. He was kind without being sentimental. He was gracious without being officious. He refused to be made into a political leader and resisted the pressure to become merely a popular hero.[49]

In the final analysis, Thurman's Christology offers insight to the contemporary church - and has implications and application - in at least three principle areas: *Imperative, Inspiration, and Integration.*

Imperative

Howard Thurman spoke to the divine and moral imperative that the church shares in seeking to eradicate racial hatred and social disintegration, and advanced the appropriation of the Christian love-ethic as foundational for constructively moving towards the realization of authentic community. Thurman asserted that God's intent is for the human family to live in community as interrelated members. Jesus came into the world to call persons back into community.

As an African American, Howard Thurman possessed a Christian faith that had been forged on the anvil of slavery, segregation, and violent forms of racial oppression. In light of this, he consistently affirmed that all humankind was bound together through their common creator. Hence, for him the fundamental tenets of love, forgiveness, and prayer were the spiritual means of addressing extant forms of oppression. In a world that is still plagued with brokenness, separation, suspicion, and deadly conflicts along racial, tribal, and ethnic lines, it remains the urgent calling of Christians to affirm that God created all persons, and that we are called to exist in peaceable and just community.

The Apostle Paul's words to the church at Ephesus speak to the contemporary challenge of the church and society, and the common and persistent hope for peace that is found in Christ:

"Christ Jesus is our peace; in his flesh he has made all groups into one and has broken down the dividing wall, that is, the hostility between us... and reconciles groups to God in one body through the cross. So then you are no longer strangers and aliens, but you are citizens with the saints and also members of the household of God, built upon the foundation of the apostles and prophets, with Christ Jesus himself as the cornerstone. In him the whole structure is joined together and grows into a holy temple in the Lord; in whom you also are built together spiritually into a dwelling place for God." (Ephesians 2:14-22)

Christ's love for all humanity was redemptive in that despite human faults and frailties, Christ willingly gave his life for us. "God demonstrated love toward us, in that while we were yet sinners, Christ died for us." (Romans 5:8) Thus, hatred and fear are overcome in the various forms that they manifest themselves in human relationships – particularly racism and ethnocentricism – through God's redemptive love in Christ, who "is our peace."

An imitation of the unconditional love revealed in the teachings and life of Jesus can be helpful in the quest for community. Moving towards a deeper sense of who we are as individuals and community will enable us to live more shalom-filled lives, modeled on the life of Christ. There is the obligation to treat every person as Christ Himself, respecting his/her life as if it were the life of Christ.

Inspiration

In *Jesus and the Disinherited,* Howard Thurman asserted that Jesus was aware of the cultural context of his ministry. Jesus knew that his teachings regarding God's justice, love, mercy, forgiveness and peace would get him into trouble. Yet, he remained faithful to his mission, and sought to perpetually live the God-inspired message that he had been given. Like Christ, Howard Thurman, as a "God intoxicated man", offered a paradigm of God-centered and God-inspired ministry. The effectiveness of Thurman's Christian witness is to be viewed in light of this God-connectedness. With Christ as the center of his word and witness, Thurman remained inspired to prophetically challenge principalities and powers of the church and society to work for peace with justice.

Howard Thurman viewed the appropriation of community as a transformational Christ-centered, Spirit-filled process that needed to be understood within the context of salvation. The development of authentic community thus requires God-connectedness through the inspiration of the Holy Spirit.

Integration

For Howard Thurman, the promise and hope of integration is at the heart of Christ's work; in Christ, human beings are sons and daughters of God, and brothers and sisters to one another. The church, the community of those who confess Christ as Lord, is an embodiment of unity within history. For this reason, the church must help the world to achieve unity, while knowing that unity among human beings is possible only if there is real justice for all. Thurman asserted that community – by its very nature - is integrative. Authentic community includes persons of different races, sexes, ages, religions, cultures, viewpoints, lifestyles, and stages of development, and serves to integrate them into a whole that is greater – more actualized and dynamic – than the sum of its parts. Forms of disintegration and disunity are, therefore, antithetical to community.

Alonzo Johnson points out that Jesus – as explicated and appropriated by Thurman – came to offer the good news of liberation to the disinherited.[50] Jesus came preaching a message of hope – a hope of peace with justice and righteousness – a radical hope that authentic community would be actualized. Amidst the hopelessness, nihilism, despair, and injustice extant in today's church and society – Jesus offers this same hope today. In the Jesus of the disinherited, evils like drugs and violence, poverty and racism are addressed. Jesus came preaching a message of hope – hope of a new creation – where as the prophet Isaiah declared:

Every valley shall be exalted,
Every mountain and hill be made low;
The uneven ground shall become level,
And the rough places made plain.
The glory of the Lord shall be revealed,
And all people shall see it together,
For the mouth of the Lord has spoken.
(Isaiah 40: 4-5)

-Chapter18-

THE AMERICAN CIVIL RIGHTS MOVEMENT: A BRIEF HISTORY AND CONTEMPORARY REFLECTIONS

(This lecture was delivered in August 2003 at the International Visitor's Program for Bulgaria Integration and Empowerment of Minorities sponsored by the Institute of International Education of the U.S. Department of Sate in Washington, DC.)

The American Civil Rights movement of the 1950s and 1960s is to be viewed against the backdrop of the history of racism in America. In 1903, African-American sociologist W. E. B. DuBois pronounced that the problem of the 20th century would be the problem of the color-line (*The Souls of Black Folk*). In 1944, Swedish sociologist Gunnar Myrdal discussed the plight of African Americans within the context of what he referred to as an "American dilemma." (*An American Dilemma: The Negro Problem and Modern Democracy*).

Thus, the struggle for Civil Rights was born out of the context of the unique and tragic racial history of America, which had its foundation in the slave trade. It was the chattel slavery of Africans brought to America's shores that served as the early foundation of the American capitalistic system, and spawned economic expansion. With the formal and legal emancipation of slaves in the 1860's, there remained a system of racism, and its incumbent economic and social oppression that continued into the early and then mid-20th century.

The Civil Rights movement is also to be seen in light of the history of the broader struggle for human rights in America. It is important to note that the United States is a country that is largely comprised of immigrant persons who arrived on these shores from across the globe. Many immigrants have come to America as the result of oppression and marginalization in their native lands. Over the course of history, Americans have dealt with issues of marginalization and oppression among many of its own. Thus, the Civil Rights movement is to be understood within the context of the struggle for rights of not only Blacks, but persons who are Jewish, Eastern European (e.g. Polish, Czech, Russian, Yugoslavian), Latino/a, and Asian (e.g. Japanese, Koreans, Vietnamese), among others. The Civil Rights movement is also to be viewed in light of the Women's Suffrage movement of the early 20th century, as women struggled for voting rights, as well as rights in the work-place in a male-dominated society.

The roots of the American Civil Rights movement can also be traced to the labor movements and unionization of the American workforce in the early twentieth century. It is important to note the role of A. Philip Randolph, a labor activist, and head of the Brotherhood of Sleeping Car Porters. Randolph played an integral role in the American Civil Rights movement by making the connections of the concerns for the rights of racial minorities and the broader concerns for equal rights among other groups in mainstream America.

The Civil Rights movement was extremely instrumental in facilitating social, economic and political change and creating an environment for moving toward equality and justice for all Americans. For African Americans, not only did they gain many legal and social rights that had previously been denied, Blacks also developed a sense of unity during this very important period in America's history. This sense of unity was primarily evidenced in the various groups that worked together for a common cause - the sense of covenant and sharing - with the prospect that real change was not an impossible dream.

In working together toward the common goals of racial equality and social justice, many black and white Americans came to the realization that instead of guns and violence, peaceful means of protest and defiance could be employed to accomplish the same goals - with the prospect of long-term progress for American society and the world.

One of the first organizations to promote a systematic non-violent approach in the effort to gain racial equality, desegregation and ultimately integration was the National Association for the Advancement of Colored People (NAACP). The NAACP was founded in 1909 by blacks and whites as the Niagra Movement, with the stated purpose of working toward equal rights for Negroes and other persons of color. The NAACP sought to end racial segregation and discrimination in every aspect of public life for all people.

In the early 1950's, the NAACP played an instrumental role in many court cases aimed at achieving desegregation of public facilities. One of the court cases that set a precedent in the quest for integration was Brown vs. the Board of Education of Topeka, Kansas. This landmark 1954 case effectively overturned the 1896 court decision in Plessy vs. Ferguson, which had established the doctrine of "separate-but-equal." The 1954 U.S. Supreme Court decision resulted in the prohibition of segregation in public schools and other public institutions.

Although Roy Wilkens, then the executive director of the NAACP, and other leaders were frequently criticized by many blacks over the issue of the role and methods of the NAACP in discrimination cases, the organization continued to organize sit-ins, picket lines, demonstrations and selective buying campaigns (boycotts) in efforts to combat racial discrimination.

In the late 1950's, new leadership began to emerge in the black community, particularly in the southern United States. Influenced by the techniques employed by the NAACP, new leaders and their respective organizations began to focus on the prospect of non-violence as their primary operational strategy.

In Montgomery, Alabama in 1955, a black woman took a seat near the front of a city bus, and refused to obey the driver's order to move to the back and let a white man sit in her seat. This was a common practice throughout the South at the time. Rosa Parks was jailed for her singular act of defiance, and blacks throughout Montgomery were outraged by her detention. Many people thought of rioting or other acts of violence as the best means to express their indignation at the treatment of Mrs. Parks.

However, black church and civic leaders in Montgomery formed the Montgomery Improvement Association to facilitate its method of nonviolent protest, and elected the Rev. Dr. Martin Luther King, Jr. as president of the organization.

The 381-day boycott of Montgomery city buses eventually led to a Supreme Court decision prohibiting racial discrimination with regard to seating in/on public accommodations. The success of the Montgomery effort served to set the stage for what would be a long array of effective peaceful demonstrations as a primary means of eradicating discriminatory practices in America.

Subsequent to the triumph in Montgomery, and with the formation of the Southern Christian Leadership Conference (SCLC) in 1957, Blacks throughout the nation began to replicate the methods of nonviolent protest that had been so effectively employed in Montgomery.

It is important to note the influence of Mohandas Gandhi, the leader of the nonviolent struggle for the rights of Indians against British rule. Martin Luther King, Jr. and others in the American Civil Rights movement essentially adopted the Hindu principles of ahimsa (non-injury) and satyagraha (truth/love/soul force) that had been successfully employed by Gandhi.

The doctrine of nonviolent resistance continued to be deployed as a means of protest throughout the 1950's and 1960's. However, with the advent of the Negro Revolt - which also came to be known as the Black Power movement - the nonviolent methods of the NAACP and SCLC began to be challenged. More militant aggregations like the Student Nonviolent Coordinating Committee (led by Stokely Carmichael, a.k.a. Kwame Toure), and the Congress of Racial Equality (led by James Foreman) began to cast doubt as to whether the slow wheels of legal action in the courtrooms, and methods of nonviolent resistance would ever fully address the root problems of racism in America.

But Martin Luther King, Jr. and the SCLC remained resolute in their approach. Despite the clearly Christian approach employed by King and others, they were constantly subjected to various forms of physical and psychological violence. Those who participated in the Civil Rights movement were jailed on numerous occasions. Homes were bombed, windows and doors were bashed, crosses were burned, and there were untold instances of police brutality, raids, fire hosing, and dog-attacks as means of intimidating those who protested nonviolently for civil rights.

None of these acts of violence seemed to dampen the spirits or weaken the resolve of those committed to the movement for equal rights through the means of nonviolent resistance. The March on Washington on August 28, 1963 is considered to be the capstone event of the Civil Rights movement. Martin Luther King, Jr. used this occasion - on the steps of the Lincoln Memorial in the Nation's Capital - to challenge America as a nation to fulfill the promise of equality and justice as outlined in the Declaration of Independence and the Constitution of the United States, and to share his dream of a society where persons "would be judged not by the color of their skin, but by the content of their character."

The March on Washington, which involved more than 250,000 people gathered together in nonviolent protest, had a significant impact on influencing political change. The March led to the passage of the Civil Rights Act of 1964, the Voting Rights Act of 1965, and the Fair Housing Act of 1968. Although the passage of these legislative measures accomplished a great deal in the progress towards racial inclusiveness in America, they have not resulted in the eradication of racism. However, these congressional acts have served as an impetus for the ongoing struggle for equal rights and opportunity.

In the mid-1960's, King began to direct his energies away from the South, and towards some of the larger cities in the northern United States. And in addition to the eradication of racism, he began to focus on the elimination of poverty and war. (Racism, poverty and militarism are what King referred to as the "triplets of evil").

With the focus of the American Civil Rights movement shifting to northern urban areas, the National Urban League, then headed by executive director Whitney M. Young, Jr., became another important organization in the struggle for civil/human rights and equality.

The National Urban League directed its efforts toward facilitating change at the local, state and federal government levels seeking to improve living and working conditions in the nation's urban areas. Even though this organization did not have explicitly strong ties to the religious community, as did the SCLC, it still focused on many of the same issues.

One of the major efforts of the National Urban League occurred in the Watts area of Los Angeles, California. In the aftermath of the Watts riots of 1965, Whitney Young and the Urban League established fifteen Head Start child development programs, as well as many other programs designed to facilitate community and economic development in Los Angeles. The National Urban League initiated similar programs in cities such as Detroit, Chicago, and Washington, DC.

Concluding Observations

A few summary observations can be made about the American Civil Rights movement. First, at the time of the assassination of Martin Luther King, Jr. in 1968, the focus of the Civil Rights movement was becoming broader with attention given not only to racial equality, but also poverty (economic justice) and war (militarism). King had begun to refer to racism, poverty and militarism as the "triplets of evil."

Second, the American Civil Rights movement influenced several contemporary movements aimed at promoting social justice, like the women's rights movement of the 1960's and 70's, the concerns for persons with dis-abilities (other-abled persons), and the focus on the rights of persons who are gay and lesbian (among others).

Third, the American Civil Rights movement can be understood in global perspective, and connections can be found in the struggle for human rights and independence in various nations in African (e.g. Ghana, South African, Zimbabwe), Eastern Europe (e.g. Poland, the former Soviet Union, the former Yugoslavia, Germany), and South America.

Fourth, the American Civil Rights movement, and the ongoing struggle for equality, must be seen/understood within the context of growing racial and ethnic diversity in the United States. Although the "problem of the color line" remains as we have moved into the 21st century, this is no longer simply a black-white concern. According to U.S. Census data, as of 2002, Hispanics are the largest ethnic minority group in the United States. African Americans are now the second largest racial-ethnic minority group. Population projections indicate that by the year 2020, there will be no racial majority group in America.

Therefore, several critical concerns seem apparent. As America lives into this growing diversity, what lessons can be learned from the historical struggles for equality and justice? How do we comprehend and live into the growing racial-ethnic diversity that is before us? What will be the political, social and cultural implications of this diversity?

-Chapter 19-

CLOSE ENCOUNTERS

(John 4)

(This sermon was first delivered at the Convocation on Multicultural Ministry, New Jersey Annual Conference, UMC in September 1999 in Newark, New Jersey.)

There is perhaps nothing more refreshing than an encounter that takes us by surprise. Such an unexpected encounter often assumes the character of enlightening the human spirit and leading towards renewed perceptions of life's meaning and purpose. We learn, through such encounters, of others, and in so doing, we learn something more about ourselves.

Often such encounters serve to thrust us into a realm that is beyond our comfort zone – into another sense of being – ultimately expanding our world-view and renewing our hope in the midst of an otherwise flawed and disjointed humanity. Thus, as uncomfortable and awkward as they might appear on the surface - there is a certain benefit – some good, some utility, that comes out of such unexpected encounters.

One such encounter remains vivid in my memory. I was an eighteen year old college freshman, and it was my first day at the University of Maryland. Having grown up mostly within the urban confines of Washington, DC, my exposure to cultures other than my own was still quite limited.

I shall never forget. On that first day of college, I was filled with excitement and anticipation about who my roommate would be. What would he look like? Would he like sports? What kind of music would he like? All of the typical concerns of a college freshman filled my curiosity.

Jerry seemed to be everything that I expected him not to be. He seemed to be everything that I wasn't. He was white and I was black. He had spent his whole life in the suburbs of New Jersey, and I had spent most of mine in the city of Washington, DC. He was Jewish, and I was Methodist.

Our encounter was a clash of cultures if there ever was one. Here we were – two eighteen year olds – suddenly thrust into the awkwardness of this close encounter. By random selection – I suppose – we had been placed in a relationship where we would have to learn of each other, and learn of ourselves in order that our common space and time could become a realm of peace and growth for both of us.

This was a close encounter for Jerry and me. Thrust - we were – into a relationship that would require that we both move beyond the "comfort zone" that each of us had known – into a new space and a new time that would become our common ground over the next few years of our lives.

The Samaritan woman written about in the fourth chapter of John's Gospel found herself in a close encounter with Jesus. I can imagine that as she encountered the Lord, it was a moment of awkwardness and even discomfort not unlike that which Jerry and I had experienced. This was a moment of awkwardness and discomfort for this woman, as well as for Jesus.

Suddenly, these two persons from very different cultures – from very distinctive backgrounds – were moved from their respective places of familiarity into a space and time of discovering new ground – common ground – holy ground.

In this close encounter, we see a cross-cultural, multicultural, multi-ethnic experience - a Samaritan woman and Jesus of Nazareth. Cross-cultural, multicultural encounters have a way, by their very nature of making us uncomfortable – wary and apprehensive about ourselves and others. By their very nature, these encounters have a way of moving us from our present reality, to new, higher and holy ground.

Upon close examination, we notice that this Samaritan woman and Jesus held something in common – something to which they could both relate out of their unique experiences and needs.

It was the water that they held in common. The water is what brought them to this common place and time. The water is that which united them. A close encounter it was.

It was the water that served to attract them to the point of this encounter. And Jesus made it plain that it was not just any water that his woman could experience, but that she could experience the living water that flows forth from Christ and Christ alone.

I believe that the multicultural experience between the Samaritan woman and Jesus of Nazareth has direct implications for the church today. Despite our differences, our distinctiveness, our points of divergence and digression – whether it is the style of worship to which we have become accustomed - the types of singing and preaching....or whether we consider ourselves urban or rural or suburban... or whether our congregations are predominantly Hispanic, Native American, Asian, black or white... or whether we are younger or older – if we have had a close encounter with Jesus – we hold something in common.

One of the commonalities that we share is the living water. The living water affirms and acclaims our common bond. We have a common baptism – even with our distinctiveness and diversity. The living water is a tie that binds us. The living water, as manifest in and through our baptism – is a tie that weaves through our multi-ethnicity – and knits us together.

What are some of the lessons that we can learn from the Samaritan woman's close encounter with Jesus of Nazareth? How might the teachings found in this discourse help us live in closer, more wholistic relationships with those who are in some ways unlike us?

A first lesson that we learn is the lesson of *intentionality*. Jesus was intentional in approaching the Samaritan woman. There were probably more reasons that he could have used not to approach her than there were reasons for approaching her.

She was a Samaritan, and he was Jewish. In a male dominated culture, Jesus could have used his cultural privilege – his maleness, as well as his Jewish status – and chosen not to speak to her – not to engage in such an encounter with this woman. And Jesus knew that this Samaritan woman was considered to be sinner in her own culture because of the number of times she had been married. There were any number of reasons why Jesus could have chosen not to deal with this woman.

But Jesus intentionally sought to establish a relationship with this Samaritan woman. Certainly, there are any number of reasons that we could use today to try to explain why multicultural relationships are difficult, if not impossible to establish. Reasons why we choose to worship with people who look and think the most like us. Reasons why we choose to live, and even shop in places where those around us look and think the way we do.

Engaging in multicultural relationships – whether in the church or society – demands of us a certain degree of intentionality; it requires recognition that it is God who wills for us to take the initiative to make a difference – even if it means that we might have to stand alone.

Secondly, we learn from the close encounter of the Samaritan woman with Jesus the lesson of *interaction.* As Jesus interacted with the Samaritan woman, he looked for ways to relate with her. He and she knew of their differences, and we might surmise that the interaction between them may have been awkward and strained.

Likewise, our encounters with those who are different may feel awkward and strained, but in order to establish relationship – in order to overcome the barriers that often serve to become "cultural protectors and security blankets" for us - it is important for us to develop effective means of interacting and communicating with each other.

Often cross-cultural communication and interaction takes a greater deal of time and more effort than we might expect, but this time and effort – this interaction and dialogue – is critical to establishing wholistic, healthy relationships across cultures.

A third lesson that we glean from this encounter is that of *invitation.* As a direct result of the Lord's intentionality and interaction with the Samaritan woman, he was able to extend to her an avenue for a deeper, more meaningful relationship. Jesus invited her into a life-changing, life-giving, eternal experience in and through him – the living water.

Once we come to know one another on more profound levels, our Christian hospitality takes the form of invitation into more meaningful, enduring, life-giving, life-changing relationships with one another. We yearn to fellowship and experience the presence of those who we come to know as our sisters and brothers in Christ. Invitation becomes less formal, and more a way of living out our faith in its fullness as we seek to experience all of the beauty of God's people. Jesus – the living water – invited the Samaritan woman into a meaningful relationship with him.

A fourth lesson learned from this close encounter is that of *imperative*. The value that ultimately predicated the actions of Jesus toward the Samaritan woman was imperative. Jesus had a profound sense of God's purpose for his life – God's divine calling to live a life that was beyond his own humanity.

It was his calling, God's imperative upon his life – as manifest through his own baptism – that led Jesus to the understanding that his Word, his love, his presence were life-giving. Jesus understood that the living water that he was, and had come to offer, was both inclusive and universal.

My prayer is that we would hear and heed God's imperative in this present day to go and make disciples of persons of all nations. O that we would hear God's word that in Christ there is no east or west, north or south. O that we would know today, that each of us who are a part of God's creation is privileged to drink from the well of the living water.

May God, who is full of grace and love – and who offered us Christ, the living water – grant us the courage and wisdom to extend lovingkindness to all of God's children, and to do justice even when our actions might seem unpopular, unfruitful, and misunderstood. And may God grant us the strength of character to always walk humbly.

-Chapter 20 –

A STRANGE ENCOUNTER: HOSPITALITY, JESUS AND THE SYROPHOENICIAN WOMAN

(Mark 7:24-30, Matthew 15:21-28)

(This sermon was first delivered as the plenary address for the Western Pennsylvania Annual Conference Service of Racial Reconciliation at Grove City College in June 2004.)

Theologian Miroslav Volf suggests that a way of understanding the ministry of Jesus is to see his practice of ministry within the context of 'double vision.' According to Volf, the biblical notion of 'double vision' involves seeing with the eyes of others, accepting their perspective, and discovering the new significance of one's own basic commitments.[51]

Our divine prerogative involves a choice of the will, whether we will decide to engage in 'double vision' – to embrace the 'other', or to exclude the 'other' that is a part of our reality. And if our choice is to embrace, and not to exclude, then what will be the quality of our embrace? On whose terms, and on whose turf, will our embrace transpire?

These are critical concerns for the church and society today. It seems to be our collective propensity to lean toward exclusion, and away from embrace. In this 50th year anniversary of the monumental Supreme Court decision, Brown vs. the Board of Education of Topeka, Kansas, which struck down the notion of "separate but equal" pertaining to schools and other public accommodations - separation, segregation, discrimination, isolation, and alienation remain incumbent in society, and within many aspects of the church's life today.

We are reminded that it was in 1903 that Dr. W.E.B DuBois, in his seminal work, *The Souls of Black Folk,* declared that "the problem of the 20th century is the problem of the color line." It seems that 101 years later, the problem of the 21st Century remains the problem of the color line. It is just the case today that the color line, as conceived by DuBois, is no longer simply black and white. Today the color line is various shades of brown, yellow, and red – comprising not only Europeans and Africans, but also Native Americans, Hispanics and Asians.

The problem of the color line is perhaps more complex in that to deal with the problem of color – race and ethnicity in America today – we are also beckoned to address issues of class, gender and sexual orientation and identity, among the other forms and shapes of diversity among us.

Amidst these forms, shapes and hues of diversity, proposals of church schism in the United Methodist Church and other denominations - though not unique to this generation - remind us, yet again of our proclivity towards division.

Our theological-religious problem seems to lie in the possibility that such division, at its core, is antithetical to what it means to be the church - both as ecclesia (at the structural level) and oikomene (the church as a universal, ecumenical entity).

Furthermore, it seems that war, territorialism, colonialism, isolationism and terrorism – though essentially societal concerns - are not to be viewed outside the context of the church's propensity toward schism, separation and segregation. In other words it should not be lost on the church that the observation of Dr. Benjamin E. Mays of several decades past rings true today, that "Sunday morning remains the most segregated hour of the week."

It seems that throughout Scripture, the biblical imperative - the divine prerogative – is that humanity – would move towards embrace, and away from exclusion – and that we would strive to appropriate inclusion, and not segregation.

Interestingly, the specific example that Miroslav Volf cites for such a divine imperative is Jesus' encounter with the Syrophoenician woman.[52]

The passage begins with Jesus moving into the region of Tyre, a move that comes directly on the heels of a discussion with religious authorities concerning the purity code as it defines proper etiquette for table fellowship.

Here, the laws regarding purity form a major barrier to the

realization of any form of authentic community. In this case, the Pharisees' objections to those with "unwashed hands" may allude to the fact that the disciples are assumed to be contaminated because they have already been eating with the gentiles and sharing their unclean foods. Jesus responds by drawing a conceptual map of purity and impurity that contrasts the external—what is put in the body—with the internal—what comes from the body. (Mark 7.21-22)

Volf points out that in and through his encounter with the Syrophoenecian woman, through 'double vision,' Jesus' understanding of his mission was enlarged, and that he gained a new insight and understanding of the 'other.'

It also seems to be the case that the Syrophoenecian woman here engages in similar 'double vision." In the exchange between them she too models seeing from a different perspective. She remains who she is - a foreign woman who worships different gods and takes the risk of acting in more than one world, of speaking more than one language. She steps outside herself and seeks to have Jesus take a similar step if only for a moment. She seeks to also have Jesus inhabit, however briefly, where she is, and who she is.

A Strange Encounter

The challenge of embrace amidst this strangeness is evident - "Sir, even the dogs under the table eat the children's crumbs." This challenge is rooted in the knowledge of her own sense of powerlessness, dislocation and oppression. This challenge is also rooted in the experience of segregation and separation because of class, gender and race, and here she seeks to redefine justice for Jesus.

She challenges Jesus to see her daughter as 'his child,' as one with a claim on his power, so that her daughter can be freed from the demon who is stealing her life. This woman asserts that if he were to deny her, and refuse to re-make her daughter, he would be complicit in the harm caused by the demon's possession of her daughter. In as much as this woman's challenge is directed at Jesus' personal conscience, it is also directed at the structural barriers – whether religious, political, or social - that had served to impede any possibility of embrace, hospitality, community, inclusion, and justice.

The Syrophoenician woman's challenge amidst this strange

encounter is a beckoning for hospitality. Hospitality is one of the constants of the biblical witness. From the account of Abraham's experience at the oaks of Mamre in Genesis 18, to Philip's interaction with the Ethiopian eunuch, we see that the theme of hospitality is woven into the sacred texts of the Christian faith. In 2 Samuel, David showed hospitality (kindness) by inviting Mephibosheth, a servant, the son of Jonathan, to dine at his royal table, and in Hebrews 13 we are reminded to be mindful of how we entertain strangers for they might be angels unknown.

In the Bible, there is hospitality to the other, the foreigner, the stranger, and the outcast; hospitality that is extended and hospitality that is received. Hospitality accompanies the biblical accounts of creation, exodus, exile, redemption, reconciliation, resurrection and restoration.

John Koening, in *New Testament Hospitality,* offers that New Testament hospitality centers upon meetings and transactions with strangers that are characterized by the shifting of guest and host roles ... The kingdom breaks in on meals and other occasions of welcoming; or it somehow advances through alliances with strangers ... The kingdom often turns out to be both cause and consequence of hospitality.[53]

Christ is ultimately an exemplar of hospitality.   In Christ, Christians claim that the host has mysteriously become the guest, and has become the guest so thoroughly that the host (Christ) put his identity at risk – his divinity at risk - through self-emptying and suffering death. For the sake of hospitality in an inhospitable world, Christ offered himself for us.

Parker Palmer, in his book *The Company of Strangers,* shares that hospitality "means valuing the strangeness of the stranger ... it means meeting the stranger's needs while allowing him or her simply to be, without attempting to make the stranger over into a modified version of ourselves." [54]

Henri Nouwen, in *Reaching Out,* asserts that the purpose of hospitality is not to change people, but to offer space where change can take place. Hospitality is not to bring women and men over to our side, but to offer freedom not disturbed by dividing lines.[55]

When Jesus healed the Syrophoenician woman's daughter, he did not insist that she move to Galilee, or that she become like the disciples. Jesus did not denigrate her status, nor extol his own.

She did not need to become like him to experience God's grace, because hospitality respects and honors both the giver and the receiver of hospitality.

How might the church live hospitably amidst the inhospitableness that seems to so define our world. These four summary affirmations regarding hospitality might serve to help shape our ongoing reflection.

First, we might affirm that hospitality is the necessary theological context in which we come to interpret those aspects of life that may seem strange and alien to us. The United Methodist Church's communications campaign, "Open Hearts, Open Minds, and Open Doors" seems to offer an intentional framework for engaging in such a process.

The common thread in this campaign is that we are to be "open." Open to what? Open to the ways in which God's spirit beckons us to engage in acts of faithfulness. We are to be open to moving beyond our boundaries and barriers. Open to engaging in acts of radical inclusiveness, and gestures of bold embrace and hospitality.

It is important to reiterate that to extend hospitality is to neither ignore nor downplay the differences and characteristics of identity. Such differences and characteristics illustrate that the kingdom of God is far greater and far more diverse than any person will ever be able to imagine. We come from the north, south, east and west to take our places at the feast in the presence of God. Nevertheless all are invited to sit at the common table; differences are not cause for division, but serve as an opportunity to celebrate how we are fearfully and wonderfully created by God.

Second, we might affirm that hospitality is the means by and through which a notion of "strong diversity" is realized in the church and society. Here, notions of "weak diversity" and "strong diversity" must be distinguished. Much of what we have become accustomed to in terms of diversity is weak diversity.

Weak diversity would say to us that "we must go along with diversity just to get along." Weak diversity would suggest that we are willing to put up with a little difference, or tolerate a little color in our midst as long as it does not upset the status quo – as long as it does not disturb our sense of comfort to any great degree – and as long as it does not result in too much structural, systemic or political change.

Strong diversity – as born through hospitality – leads us towards a sense of the valuation of the other. We not only tolerate the other, but we value the other because we come to know that the other is a part of the "I." Strong diversity is an appropriation of the African philosophical notion that "I am because we are, and because we are, therefore, I am."

Third, we might affirm that hospitality is the means by which community as God's teleos - God's purpose, God's ideal - is realized. Community becomes a reality through hospitality. Hospitality leads us towards a movement away from mere exterior, sentimental contact - and towards authentic contextualization and integration with, and for, one another.

God created us to be community, and that which violates this divine prerogative – terror, war, segregation, violence in any form - is sinful. This is what Dr. Martin Luther King, Jr. often alluded to in his notion of _"Beloved Community."_ King pointed out that we who comprise the world are a part of an inextricable web of inclusion. God created the universe in a way that all that is, is interrelated, interdependent and interconnected. God's purpose for us is to be community.

Fourth, (finally), we might affirm that hospitality is the means by and through which we begin to re-imagine, re-vision, re-new, re-name, re-frame and re-make that which has been, and is our reality. We do not necessarily disclaim our current reality, who we are, what we value and sense is important - but a process of 'double visioning' helps us to live into diversity and otherness not with fear, but with wonder.

This is the vision of Pentecost. At Pentecost, God pours out God's Spirit on the church and society, and we are able to "dream new dreams and see new visions."

Indeed, to live hospitably is to envision, imagine, hope, and dream for a future where we celebrate our common giftedness, and our common faith in Christ.

-Chapter 21 -

RECOVERING A SENSE OF HISTORY

(1 Kings 18:30-40)

(This sermon was first presented at the Black History Month worship service at Wesley Theological Seminary in February 2005.)

It is very apparent that one of the greatest tragedies of this present age is that too many people have lost a sense of their history. Across virtually all spectrums of society – whether we are younger or older, black or white, rich or poor - people have lost a sense of history. And the danger comes in that to lose a sense of our history is to forget from whence we have come. And when we forget from whence we have come, we fall into the trap of not knowing where we are going.

We've lost a sense of history. And in the midst of this, we've lost our spiritual and communal bearings. And thus we are - in large measure - out of alignment with God and with each other. This is evident in how loneliness, separation and segregation have overtaken our sense of being. Almost everybody seems to be out for themselves. We're out of alignment with God and with each other.

Many people don't know who they are or whose they are. And so we look for meaning, relevance and purpose in all the wrong places. We seek to find ourselves in drugs and alcohol, in make-up and make-overs, in money and status, and in people who may not love us for who we are, but want us for what we can do for them.

We've lost our sense of history. Hip-hop, and other forms of popular music, art and culture, that too often glorify greed, demean and misogynize women, and promote violence seem to have permeated the very depths of our reality.

It seems that too many people have forgotten the struggles

of those who endured the devastation of the middle passage, and the atrocities of slavery, the anguish of Jim Crow, the despair of depression, and the struggles for Civil Rights. We've lost a sense of our history.

We've forgotten the stories, the struggles and the strength of those "sheroes" and heroes like Fannie Lou Hammer, Sojourner Truth, and Harriett Tubman. We've forgotten about those like Richard Allen, Martin Luther King, Jr. and Thurgood Marshall who paved the way for us.

In March 2003, I returned to Madison Heights, Virginia, just outside of Lynchburg, Virginia to eulogize my maternal Grandmother Dorothy Mae Parrish, who had passed away at the age of 83 years old. In preparing for what I was going to say about my grandmother's life and legacy, many memories emerged of my growing up and spending time on Sunset Drive in Madison Heights as a young boy.

Indeed, my preparation of this eulogy was not simply a time of preparing to preach, but these were moments filled with nostalgia and reminiscence. These were also moments of giving thanks for the lessons that I'd received on the porch of my grandmother and other relatives on Sunset Drive.

As never before, I came to a sense of profound appreciation for the lessons of faith and life that my Grandmother Dorothy and Grandfather William had taught me. I also began to give God thanks for the lessons taught by my paternal grandparents, Vicie and Charles Hunt, in Maryland. I thought about my Great-grandparents – several of whom I was privileged to know and glean lessons of life from.

In preparing to preach my grandmother's eulogy, I had come to the profound realization that those wise relatives on Sunset Drive in Virginia, and those in Maryland and in North Carolina had been some of my best teachers. Although I have had the privilege – over the course of my formal education - to study at some of the finest universities in the land, it was on the porches and at the dinner tables of my grandparents, my uncles and aunts, and my cousins that I have learned the most.

I realized that although I have been the beneficiary of a first-tier theological education – I have studied the theological disciplines, worked with some of the world's leading theologians, and have become well-respected as a pastor and professor – it was within the hallowed walls of Rose Chapel Baptist Church – under the wise tutelage of my great-grandmother Lena Wood – in her primary and intermediate Sunday School classes – that I gained the most knowledge about the ways of God.

And I realized that it was within the old, tattered walls of St. Paul United Methodist Church and Gibbons United Methodist Church where these lessons were reinforced, and I was blessed with a faith that continues to sustain me to this day.

As we reflect on 1 Kings, we see how the Prophet Elijah found himself leading God's people through an exercise in recapturing a sense of their history. Their sense of history had been challenged by new gods and new religious realities that had come into their midst.

Indeed, we see clearly here that when history is challenged, there is a threat to any sense of identity, and being into the future.

These new forms of religious practice – as embodied in the worship of Baal - threatened Israel's sense of identity, and thus its future. Its hopes, its dreams, and its very destiny were at stake.

I remember that one of the most important history lessons that my elders taught me was to "never forget from whence you have come." This was connected with the admonition that wherever you go in life, "never forget who you are, and whose you are."

Israel had forgotten who they were, and whose they were (they found themselves in an identity crisis). And so Elijah said to all the people "Come closer to me." The people needed reminders of from whence they had come. And furthermore they needed reminders of who they were, and whose they were. They needed a history lesson. They needed to regain their spiritual bearings. They needed to get back in alignment with God.

Their destiny was at stake. And so they needed to remember who it was who had brought them to the point where they were. How did they get to where they were?

- It was the God of Israel who had called them and kept them, through Abraham, Isaac and Jacob.
- It was God who had helped them endure Egyptian slavery, and delivered them at the Red Sea.

- It was God who had again helped them endure and find their way in the wilderness, and helped them get to the Promised Land.

And so it was in the context of this same God that Elijah gathered the people, and then proceeded to repair the altar of the Lord that had been thrown down.

And then Elijah took twelve stones, according to the number of tribes of the sons of Jacob, and with the stones Elijah built another altar in the name of the Lord.

With these stones and at this altar Elijah was trying to help the people of Israel recapture a sense of their history. These stones point to at least three aspects of history.

- *Story* – These stones reminded the people of their story. These were reminders of how God had blessed them in the past, and would bless them in the future.
- *Struggle* – These stones reminded them of their struggle. Any faith story is not complete without struggle. It was in the midst of their struggles that God had blessed their lives. It seems that so often, God's people today don't have a sense of what it means to struggle. We want success without struggle. We want a crown without the cross. We are reminded of the words of Frederick Douglas who once intimated that "there can be no progress without struggle."
- *Strength* – These stones were finally evidence of God's strength in the midst of all that they had been struggling through. It's good to know that as Elijah had prepared the context for worship, God showed up in a fire, and consumed all that had been offered before God.

And when the people saw the miracle-working power of God in their midst, they were amazed. They fell on their faces, and declared, "The Lord indeed is God." "The Lord indeed is God."

As we press forward in history to the life of Jesus, it's good to know that Jesus had a sense of history. We recall that as he entered into public ministry, the Lord went into the synagogue, and he picked up a scroll and began reading words recorded in the book of Isaiah (over 700 years prior):

The Spirit of the Lord is upon me...
Because God has anointed me
To bring good news to the poor
God has sent me to proclaim release to the captives
And recovery of sight to the blind
To let the oppressed go free
To proclaim the acceptable year of the Lord. (Luke 4:18-19)

A sense of history. It is our task never to forget our story... our struggle ... and our strength...

Blessed Assurance ... Jesus is mine
O what a foretaste ... Of glory divine
Heir of salvation ... Purchase of God.
Born of his Spirit ...Washed in his blood.
This is my story ... This is my song.
Praising my savior ... All the day long.
This is my story ... This is my song.
Praising my savior ... All the day long.

-Chapter 22-

AND YET THE MELODY LINGERS

(PSALM 137:1-6)

(This sermon was first delivered as the black history month address in February 2000 at Wesley Theological Seminary in Washington, DC.)

Several years ago, the popular singing group, "Earth, Wind and Fire" recorded a song in which the title encouraged us to "Sing a Song."

"If you feel down and out…
    Sing a song…
        It'll make your day…"

Indeed, there is something about the melodious music that we sing that serves to soothe our hearts, and lift our spirits. A good song can offer hope in despair, and bring us joy in sadness. A good song can make our day.

And if there is anything that we - the people of the African Diaspora - share in common – it is that we are a singing people. If there is any one thing that defines African people, it is our ability and willingness to sing. That has been our stamp, our mark - that we are a singing people.

Almost one hundred years ago, renown sociologist, Dr. W.E.B. DuBois, in his classic work, *The Souls of Black Folk*, shared that black people have offered three significant gifts to American life as a whole – (1) the gift of the sweat and brawn; (2) the gift of the spirit; and (3) the gift of the song and story.

We are a people of the song – a people of the rhythm - a people of the beat. Whether in the church or at a party, we have had a song to sing. Whether in the great cathedrals of the land, or the best of concert halls, it has been well-known that African peoples are people of the song. Whether the spirituals or the blues, jazz or gospel, hip-hop or reggae, we have been a singing people.

What would impress any person in travels to the various corners of the earth is that African people wherever we are physically located - and whatever our lot - are a singing people. Whether in Mutare, Zimbabwe, or Capetown, South Africa, Ghana or Sierra Leonne on the western shores of the African continent, it is evident that we are a singing people. In the Caribbean or Central and South America, or in any Black neighborhood in the United States, it is clear that African people are singing people.

It is the song that has sustained and nurtured us. It is the song that has offered hope and engendered joy. The song has been the source of our spiritual pharmacology – our elixir – our balm – healing the ills and hurts, the wounds and disease of this sin-sick world.

The Psalm writer reminds us of the predicament of the Israelites in Psalm 137. Here they are, trapped in bondage by the rivers of Babylon... trapped in a strange land. And in their desperation the Israelites ask a question, "How do we sing the Lord's song in a strange land?"

The Israelites (here) found themselves in no mood to sing. How were they to sing in the midst of adversity? They were in no mood to sing ... trouble all around them... no hope and no joy. How were they supposed to sing the Lord's song?

The turbulent and tempestuous nature of contemporary life can lead us to ponder this very same matter in the year 2000. How do we keep singing... and keep worshipping... and keep praising the Lord... and keep trusting in Jesus in the midst of adversity?

How do we sing in the midst of abject poverty and virulent racism? How do we sing in the midst of suffering and sickness? How can we sing amidst violence and death, where too many of our young people are dying on our streets? How do we sing the Lord's song?

You see there's something I've come to realize about singing the Lord's song. It's easy to sing when life is rosy and cozy. It's not hard to sing when the bills are paid, and good health abounds. It's easy to sing amidst comfort and convenience.

But the true challenge of singing comes amidst the "strange land" situations of life. The challenge comes when the nights are darkest, and even the days are dim. When there is no money in the bank. When sickness and death visit our lives. When it seems that loved ones have forsaken us. When it seems that we've done all that we can do to stand.

This is why we need to take time every now and then to be reminded of the importance of our perpetual song. We will all face strange land situations in life. There will be times for all of us when we find ourselves beside the proverbial "Rivers of Babylon."

There will be times when we feel separated and segregated from God, and from one another. Times of lostness and alienation. Times of desperation and disillusionment. It is in the strange lands – at the banks of Babylon - that we need to have the capacity to keep on singing.

And we need to know that it's all right from time to time to ask the question, "How can we sing God's song?" It's all right to talk to the Lord. For to ask the question indicates that we are still in conversation with God. To ask the question indicates that we are still seeking and searching for the Lord to help us sing even though we may not feel like singing.

To ponder the question "how," is to acknowledge - at the depths of our souls - that we may be bent, but we are not yet broken. We may be hurting but we know that healing is possible. We may feel a little helpless now, but we know that if we hold on – our help is on the way. It's all right to ask, "How do we keep on singing?"

The real problem comes not in asking the question of "How do we sing?" The real problem comes when we stop singing altogether. The real problem comes when we feel that there is no use in singing. The real predicament lies at the moment when we sense that we may as well throw in the towel, give up, and stop singing. The problem really is evident when we stop singing the Lord's song.

And so, we have to keep on singing. I think those who sang the blues, like Billie Holiday, Bessie Smith and B.B King were really helping us to understand that whatever the circumstance… whatever the predicament, we have to keep on singing. Whatever blows have been directed our way, we need to keep on singing.

And I'm glad that persons of faith like Dr. Thomas Dorsey, Dr. Charles Albert Tinley, Dr. Mattie Moss Clark, Rev. Shirley Ceasar, and Rev. James Cleveland were so inspired to take the blues and turn it into Gospel Music. They knew that despite the blues, it was incumbent upon African people to keep on singing.

And so Tinley could sing:
> When the storms of life are raging
> (Lord) stand by me…
> When the storms of life are raging
> Stand by me
> When the world is tossing me
> Like a ship upon the sea
> Thou who rulest wind and water
> Stand by me…

And Dorsey could sing:
> Precious Lord …Take my hand
> Lead me on …Let me stand
> I am tired … I am weak … I am worn
> Through the storm … through the night
> Lead me on … to the light
> Take my hand … Precious Lord
> Lead me home.

And then Cleveland could come along later and declare:
> I don't feel no ways tired
> I've come too far from where I started from
> Nobody told me that the road would be easy
> I don't believe (God) brought (us) this far to leave (us)…

We are encouraged today to keep on singing. If there is anything that we have learned over our almost 400 years on these American shores, it is that we have to keep on singing. Yes, physical diseases like AIDS, hypertension and diabetes continue to plague many of our people – but we have to keep on singing. Drugs are poisoning many of our people – but we have to keep on singing. Guns and violence afflict our communities – but we have to keep on singing.

I've come to remind us that through it all, the melody lingers.

- We can keep singing because we know that there's a balm in Gilead that makes the wounded whole.
- We can keep singing because we know that over our heads there's music in the air (and there must be a God somewhere).
- We can keep singing because we know that in the song, God is preparing to bless us yet again.

The melody lingers.
How can I keep singing?

> I've seen the lightning flashing
> And heard the thunder roll
> I've felt sin's breaker's dashing
> Which tried to conquer my soul

(How can we keep on singing?)

> I've heard the voice of my Savior
> He bid me still to fight on
> He promised never to leave me
> Never to leave me alone.

NOTES ON SECTON THREE

[1] Alton Pollard, *Mysticism and Social Change: The Social Witness of Howard Thurman,* (New York: Peter Lang, 1992), 3.

[2] Michael I. N. Dash, et. al. *Hidden Wholeness: An African American Spirituality for Individuals and Communities (*Cleveland, OH: United Church Press), 1.

[3] Howard Thurman, *For the Inward Journey* (Richmond, IN: Friend United Press, 1984), x.

[4] Lerone Bennett, Jr. "Eulogy of Howard Thurman: Tributes to Genius," *The African American Pulpit,* (Valley Forge, PA: Judson, Winter, 2001) p. 63, Bennett made reference to Thurman's perspective on life and personal identity at Thurman's funeral in 1981.

[5] Howard Thurman, This prayer appears in the *United Methodist Hymnal* (Nashville: United Methodist Publishing, 1989), 401.

[6] Howard Thurman, *Disciplines of the Spirit* (Richmond, IN: Friends United Press, 1987), 9.

[7] Howard Thurman, *Deep River and the Negro Spiritual Speaks of Life and Death* (Richmond, IN: Friends United Press, 1975), Thurman's thoughts on the river as metaphor for life and meaning is explicated throughout.

[8] Howard Thurman, *For the Inward Journey* (Richmond, IN: Friends United Press, 1984), 64.

[9] Howard Thurman, *Meditations of the Heart* (Richmond, IN: Friend United Press, 1953), 15.

[10] Luther Smith, *Howard Thurman: The Mystic as Prophet* (Richmond, IN: Friends United Press, 1978), 23-24.

[11] George Cross, *What is Christianity: A Study of Rival Interpretations* (Chicago: University of Chicago Press, 1918), 187.

[12] Ibid., 193.

[13] George Cross, *Christian Salvation: A Modern Interpretation* (Chicago: University of Chicago Press, 1925), 133.

[14] Ibid., 33.

[15] Roberta Byrd Barr, interview with Howard Thurman, Seattle, Washington, January 1969.

[16] Mary E. Goodwin, "Racial Roots and Religion: An Interview with Howard Thurman," *The Christian Century,* 9 May 1973, 533.

[17] Elizabeth Yates, *Howard Thurman: Portrait of a Practical Dreamer* (New York: John Day, 1964), 23.

[18] Wayne A. Meeks, *The Writings of St. Paul* (New York: Norton,

1978), xiv.

[19] Goodwin, 534.

[20] Smith, 107.

[21] Ibid., 62.

[22] See Thurman, *Jesus and the Disinherited* (Richmond, IN: Friends United Press, 1969), 89-109.

[23] Olin Moyd, *Sacred Art*, 22.

[24] Lerone Bennett, Jr. "Eulogy of Howard Thurman: Tributes to Genius," p. 63.

[25] Smith, 202.

[26] Greg Moses, *Revolution of Conscience: Martin Luther King, Jr. and the Philosophy of Nonviolence* (New York: Guilford Press, 1997), p. 151.

[27] Thurman, *Disciplines of the Spirit, 122.*

[28] Howard Thurman, *Deep is the Hunger: Meditations for Apostles of Sensitiveness* (New York: Harper and Brothers, 1951), 109.

[29] Smith, 50.

[30] See Thurman, *Disciplines of the Spirit,* 104-127.

[31] Howard Thurman, *The Search for Common Ground: An Inquiry into the Basis of Man's Experience of Community* (Richmond, IN: Friends United Press, 1971), 104.

[32] Smith, 107.

[33] Ibid.

[34] Thurman, *Jesus and the Disinherited,* 74.

[35] See Howard Thurman's analysis of hate (hatred) in *Jesus and the Disinherited,* 77-78.

[36] Thurman, *Jesus and the Disinherited*, 89.

[37] Ibid.

[38] Ibid., 89-90.

[39] Smith, 48.

[40] Thurman, *Disciplines of the Spirit,* 104-105.

[41] Thurman, *The Mood of Christmas* (Richmond, IN: Friends United Press, 1969), 19.

[42] Thurman, *Jesus and the Disinherited*, 92.

[43] Smith, 133. Luther Smith makes reference to Thurman's "Peace Tactics and a Racial Minority," *The World Tomorrow,* December, 1928, 505-507.

[44] Ibid., 51.

[45] Thurman, *The Mood of Christmas,* 9.

[46] Smith, 93.

[47] Dietrich Bonhoeffer, *Meditations on the Cross* (Louisville, KY: Westminster John Knox Press, 1996), p. 64.

[48] See Thurman, *Deep River and the Negro Spiritual Speaks of Life and Death*. Throughout, Thurman explicates the role of the Negro spiritual and other expressions of black religion as means of survival for slaves.

[49] Thurman, *The Mood of Christmas*, 9.

[50] See Alonzo Johnson, *Good News for the Disinherited: Howard Thurman on Jesus of Nazareth and Human Liberation* (New York: University Press of America, 1997.) Johnson provides a detailed treatment and explication of Thurman's Christology, with liberation as the defining motif of Christ's mission and ministry.

[51] Miroslav Volf, *Exclusion and Embrace: A Theological Exploration of Identity, Otherness and Reconciliation* (Nashville: Abingdon, 1996). Volf explicates the notion of "double vision" throughout this work.

[52] Ibid.

[53] John Koening, *New Testament Hospitality: Partnership with Strangers as Promise and Mission* (Philadelphia: Fortress Press, 1985), 124-25.

[54] Parker Palmer, *The Company of Strangers: Christianity and Renewal of America's Public Life* (New York: Crossroad Publishing Company, 1986), 68.

[55] Henri Nouwen, *Reaching Out: Three Movements of the Spiritual Life* (New York: Image Books, 1975), 71.

BIBLIOGRAPHY

Achebe, Chinua. *Things Fall Apart.* New York: Anchor Books, 1959.

Ansbro, John J. *Martin Luther King, Jr.: The Making of a Mind.* Maryknoll, NY: Orbis Books, 1982.

Ansbro, John J. *Martin Luther King, Jr.: Nonviolent Strategies and Tactics for Social Change.* Maryknoll, NY: Orbis Books, 2000.

Baker-Fletcher, Garth. *Somebodyness: Martin Luther King, Jr. and the Theory of Dignity.* Minneapolis, Fortress Press, 1993.

Baldwin, Lewis V. *There is a Balm in Gilead: The Cultural Roots of Martin Luther King, Jr.* Minneapolis: Fortress Press, 1991.

Baldwin, Lewis V. *To Make the Wounded Whole: The Cultural Legacy of Martin Luther King, Jr.* Minneapolis: Fortress Press, 1993.

Baldwin, Lewis V. and Horace Wallace. *Touched by Grace: Black Methodism in the United Methodist Chruch.* Nashville: Graded Press, 1986.

Battle, Michael. *Reconciliation: The UBUNTU Theology of Desmond Tutu.* Cleveland, OH: Pilgrim Press, 1997.

Bonhoeffer, Dietrich. *The Cost of Discipleship.* New York: Collier Books, 1949, First published in 1937.

Brueggemann, Walter. *Living Towards a Vision: Biblical Reflections on Shalom.* New York: United Church Press, 1976.

Brueggemann, Walter. *The Prophetic Imagination.* Minneapolis: Fortress Press, 1978.

Caldwell, Gilbert H. *Race, Racism and Reconciliation.* Philadelphia: Simon, 1989.

Carson, Clayborne, ed. *The Papers of Martin Luther King, Jr., Volume I: Called to Serve.* Berkley CA: University of California Press, 1992.

Carson, Clayborne, ed. *The Papers of Martin Luther King, Jr., Volume II: Rediscovering Precious Values.* Berkley, CA: University of California Press, 1994.

Carson, Clayborne, ed. *The Papers of Martin Luther King, Jr., Volume III: Birth of a New Age.* Berkley, CA: University of California Press, 1997.

Carson, Clayborne, ed. *The Papers of Martin Luther King, Jr., Volume IV: Symbol of the Movement.* Berkley, CA: University of California Press, 2000.

Carson, Clayborne, ed. *The Papers of Martin Luther King, Jr., Volume V: Threshold of a New Decade.* Berkley, CA: University of California Press, 2004.

Cone, James H. *A Black Theology of Liberation*. New York: J. B. Lippincott Co, 1970.

Cone, James H. *God of the Oppressed*. New York: Seabury Press, 1975.

Cone, James H. *The Spirituals and the Blues*. Maryknoll, NY: Orbis, 1972.

Dennis, Marie, Joseph Nangle, Cynthia Moe-Lobeda and Stuart Taylor. *St. Francis and the Foolishness of God*. New York: Orbis Books, 1993.

DuBois, W. E. B. *The Souls of Black Folk*. Chicago: A. C. McClurg & Co., 1903.

Dyson, Michael Eric. *I May Not Get There With You: The True Martin Luther King, Jr.* New York: Free Press, 2000.

Ellis, Anne Leo, ed. *First, We Must Listen*. New York: Friendship Press, 1996.

Elmer, Duane. *Cross-Cultural Conflict: Building Relationships for Effective Ministry*. Downers Grove, IL: InterVarsity Press, 1993.

Erskine, Noel Leo. *King Among the Theologians*. Cleveland, OH: Pilgrim Press, 1994.

Felder, Cain Hope. *Troubling Biblical Waters: Race, Class and Family*. Maryknoll, NY: Orbis, 1989.

Fitts, Leroy. *A History of Black Baptists..* Nashville: Broadman Press, 1985.

Fitzgerald, Kelley, ed. *Racism: The Church's Unfinished Agenda – A Journal of the National United Methodist Convocation on Racism*. Washington, DC: The United Methodist Church, General Commission on Religion and Race, 1987.

Fluker, Walter Earl. *They Looked For a City: A Comparative Analysis of the Ideal of Community in the Thought of Howard Thurman and Martin Luther King, Jr.* New York: University Press of America, 1989.

Fluker, Walter Earl and Catherine Tumber, eds. *A Strange Freedom: The Best of Howard Thurman on Religious Experience and Public Life*. Boston: Beacon Books, 1998.

Foster, Charles R. *Embracing Diversity*. Washington, DC: Alban Institute, 1997.

Foster, Charles R. and Theodore Brelsford. *We are the Church Together: Cultural Diversity in Congregational Life*. Valley Forge, PA: Trinity Press International, 1996.

Franklin, John Hope and Alfred A. Moss, Jr. *From Slavery to Freedom: A History of African Americans*. New York: McGraw Hill, 1994.

Franklin, Robert M. *Liberating Visions: Human Fulfillment and Social Justice in African American Thought*. Minneapolis: Fortress Press, 1990.

Frazier, E. Franklin. *The Negro Church in America.* New York: Schocken Books, 1963.

Gandhi, Mohandas K. *The Way to God.* Berkley, CA: Berkley Hills Books, 1999.

Garrow, David J. *Bearing the Cross: Martin Luther King, Jr. and the Southern Christian Leadership Conference.* New York: Quill, 1986.

Gates, Henry Louis. *Colored People.* New York: Harper, 1997.

Gaustad, Edwin S., ed. *A Documentary History of Religion in America, Since 1865.* Grand Rapids, MI: Eerdmans Publishing, 1993.

Griggs, Lewis Brown and Lente-Louise Louw. *Valuing Diversity: New Tools for a New Reality.* New York: McGraw Hill, 1995.

Gutierrez, Gustavo. *On Job: God-Talk and the Suffering of the Innocent.* Maryknoll, NY: Orbis Books, 1985.

Gutierrez, Gustavo. *A Theology of Liberation.* Maryknoll: NY: Orbis Books, 1971.

Gutierrez, Gustavo. *We Drink from Our Own Wells: The Spiritual Journey of a People.* Maryknoll, NY: Orbis Books, 1984.

Harding, Vincent. *Hope and History: Why We Must Share the Story of the Movement.* Maryknoll: New York: Orbis, 1990.

Hunt, C. Anthony. *Blessed are the Peacemakers: A Theological Analysis of the Thought of Howard Thurman and Martin Luther King, Jr.* Lima, OH: Wyndham Hall Press, 2005.

Hunt, C. Anthony. "The Search for Peaceful Community: A Comparative Analysis of the Thought of Howard Thurman and Martin Luther King, Jr." Ph.D. dissertation. South Bend, IN: The Graduate Theological Foundation/Oxford University (UK), 2001.

Hunt, C. Anthony. *Upon the Rock: A Model for Ministry with Back Families.* Lima, OH: Wyndham Hall Press, 2001. (Previously published as *The Black Family: The Church's Role in the African American Community.* Bristol, IN: Wyndham Hall Press, 2000.)

Ivory, Luther D. *Toward a Theology of Radical Involvement: The Theological Legacy of Martin Luther King, Jr.* Nashville, TN: Abingdon, 1997.

Johnson, Alonzo. *Good News for the Disinherited: Howard Thurman on Jesus of Nazareth and Human Liberation.* New York: University Press of America, 1997.

Jones, E. Stanley. *Gandhi: Portrayal of a Friend.* Nashville: Abingdon, 1948.

Kapur, Sudarshan. *Raising Up a Prophet: The African American Encounter with Gandhi.* Boston: Beacon Press, 1992.

King, Bernice A. *Hard Questions: Heart Answers.* New York: Broadway Books, 1997.

King, Coretta Scott, *My Life with Martin Luther King, Jr.* New York: Holt, Reinhart, and Winston, 1969.

King, Martin Luther, Jr. "A Comparison of the Conceptions of God in the Thinking of Paul Tillich and Henry Nelson Wieman." Ph.D. dissertation. Boston, MA: Boston University, 1955.

King, Martin Luther, Jr. *The Measure of a Man.* Philadelphia: Fortress Press, 1988.

King, Martin Luther, Jr. *Strength to Love.* New York: Harper & Row, 1963.

King, Martin Luther, Jr. *Stride Toward Freedom: The Montgomery Story.* New York: Harper & Row, 1958.

King, Martin Luther, Jr. *The Trumpet of Conscience.* New York: Harper & Row, 1967.

King, Martin Luther, Jr. *Where Do We Go From Here: Chaos or Community?* New York: Harper & Row, 1967.

King, Martin Luther, Jr. *Why We Can't Wait.* New York: HarperCollins, 1963.

Law, Eric H. F. *The Bush Was Burning, But Not Consumed.* St. Louis, MO: Chalice Press, 1996.

Law, Eric H. F. *The Wolf Shall Dwell with the Lamb: A Spirituality for Leadership in a Multicultural Community.* St. Louis, MO: Chalice Press, 1993.

Law, Eric H. F. *Inclusion: Making Room for Grace.* St. Louis, MO: Chalice Press, 1999.

Lebacqz, Karen. *Justice in an Unjust World.* Minneapolis: Augsburg Publishing House, 1987.

Lerner, Michael and Cornel West. *Jews and Blacks: Let the Healing Begin.* New York: Grosset Putnam, 1995.

Lincoln, C. Eric. *The Black Church Since Frazier.* New York: Schocken Books, 1974.

Lincoln, C. Eric. *Coming Through the Fire: Surviving Race and Place in America.* Durham, NC: Duke University Press, 1996.

Lincoln, C. Eric. *Martin Luther King: A Profile.* New York: Hill & Wang, 1970.

Lincoln, C. Eric. *Race, Religion and the Continuing American Dilemma.* New York:Hill & Wang, 1984.

Lincoln, C. Eric and Lawrence Mamiya. *The Black Church in the African-American Experience.* Durham, NC: Duke University Press, 1990.

Lovin, Robin, et al. *Creating a New Community: God's People Overcoming Racism.* Nashville: Graded Press, 1989.

Lyght, Ernest S. *The Religious and Philosophical Foundations in the Thought of Martin Luther King, Jr.* New York: Vantage Press,

1972.

Macquarrie, John. *Christian Unity and Christian Diversity.* London: SCM Press, 1975.

Marable, Manning. *Race, Reform, and Rebellion: The Second Reconstruction in Black America: Problems in Race, Political Economy, and Society.* Boston: South End Press, 1983.

Mathabane, Mark. *Kaffir Boy: The True Story of a Black Youth's Coming of Age in Apartheid South Africa.* New York: Plume, 1986.

McClain, William B. *Black People in the United Methodist Church: Whither Thou Goest?* Nashville: Abingdon, 1990.

McClain, William B. *Travelling Light.* New York: Friendship Press, 1981.

McClendon, James Wm. *Biography as Theology.* Philadelphia: Trinity Press International, 1974.

Merton, Thomas. *Contemplation in a World of Action.* Notre Dame, IN: University of Notre Dame Press, 1998.

Merton, Thomas. *Faith and Violence: Christian Teaching and Christian Practice.* Notre Dame, IN: University of Notre Dame Press, 1968.

Merton, Thomas. *The Nonviolent Alternative (*Revised edition of *Thomas Merton on Peace).* New York: Farrar, Straus and Giroux, 1980.

Metzger, Bruce M. and Roland E. Murphy, eds. *The New Oxford Annotated Bible with the Apocryphal/Deuterocanonical Books (New Revised Standard Version).* New York: Oxford University Press, 1991.

Mitchell, Mozella Gordon. "The Dynamics of Howard Thurman's Relationship to Literature and Theology." Ph.D. dissertation. Atlanta: Emory University, 1983.

Mitchell, Mozella Gordon. *Spiritual Dynamics of Howard Thurman's Theology.* Bristol, IN: Wyndham Hall Press, 1985.

Moyd, Olin P. *Redemption in Black Theology.* Valley Forge, PA: Judson Press, 1979.

Niebuhr, H. Richard. *Christ and Culture.* New York: Haprer & Row, 1951.

Niebuhr, Reinhold. *Moral Man and Immoral Society.* New York: Scribner, 1933.

Nouwen, Henri J. M. *The Path of Peace.* New York: Crossroad, 1995.

Oates, Stephen B. *Let the Trumpet Sound: A Life of Martin Luther King, Jr.* New York: HarperPerennial, 1982.

Panikkar, Raimundo. *The Unknown Christ in Hinduism.* Revised edition. Maryknoll, NY: Orbis Books, 1982.

Paris, Peter. *The Social Teaching of the Black Churches.* Minneapolis: Fortress Press, 1988.

Pollard, Alton B., III. *Mysticism and Social Change: The Social Witness of Howard Thurman.* New York: Lang, 1992.

Rauschenbusch, Walter. *Christianity and the Social Crisis.* New York; Harper & Row, 1907.

Recinos, Harold J. *Jesus Weeps: Global Encounters on Our Doorstep.* Nashville: Abingdon, 1992.

Recinos, Harold J. *Who Comes in the Name of the Lord: Jesus at the Margins.* Nashville: Abingdon, 1997.

Reid, Stephen Breck. *Listening In: A Multicultural Reading of the Psalms.* Nashville:Abingdon, 1997.

Schneier, Marc. *Shared Dreams: Martin Luther King, Jr. and The Jewish Community.* Woodstock, VT: Jewish Lights, 1999.

Shannon, William H. *Seeds of Peace: Contemplation and Non-Violence.* New York: Crossroad Publishing, 1996.

Smith, Kenneth L. and Ira Zepp, Jr.. *Search for the Beloved Community: The Thinking of Martin Luther King, Jr.* Valley Forge, PA: Judson Press, 1974, 1998.

Smith, Luther E., Jr. *Howard Thurman: The Mystic as Prophet.* Richmond, Indiana: Friends United Press, 1991.

Sobrino, Jon. *Spirituality of Liberation: Toward Political Holiness.* Maryknoll: Orbis Books, 1988.

Solle, Dorothy. *Suffering.* Philadelphia: Fortress Press, 1975.

Solle, Dorothee. *Thinking About God: An Introduction to Theology.* Philadelphia: Trinity Press, 1990.

Sowell, Thomas S. *Race and Culture: A World View.* New York: Basic Books, 1994.

Spencer, Jon Michael. *Protest and Praise: Sacred Music of Black Religion.* Minneapolis: Fortress Press, 1990.

Steele, Shelby. *The Content of Our Character: A New Vision for Race in America.* New York: HarperPerennial, 1990.

Stewart, Carlyle Fielding, III. "A Comparative Analysis of Theological-Ontological and Ethical Method in the Theologies of James H. Cone and Howard Thurman." Ph.D. dissertation. Evanston, IL: Northwestern University, 1982.

Stewart, Carlyle Fielding, III. *God, Being and Liberation: A Comparative Analysis of the Theologies of James Cone and Howard Thurman.* Lanham, MD: University Press, 1989.

Tatum, Beverly Daniel. *"Why are all the Black Kids Sitting Together in the Cafeteria?" And other Conversations about Race.* New York: Basic Books, 1997.

Thomas, James S. *Methodism's Racial Dilemma: The Story of the Central Jurisdiction.* Nashville: Abingdon, 1992.

Thurman, Howard. *Apostles of Sensitiveness.* Boston: American Unitarian Association, 1956.

Thurman, Howard. *The Centering Moment.* Richmond, IN: Friends United Press, 1969.

Thurman, Howard. *The Creative Encounter: An Interpretation of Religion and The Social Witness.* Richmond, IN: Friends United Press, 1954.

Thurman, Howard. *Deep is the Hunger: Meditations for Apostles of Sensitiveness.* New York: Harper and Brothers, 1951.

Thurman, Howard. *Deep River: An Interpretation of Negro Spirituals.* Mills College, CA: Eucalyptus Press, 1945.

Thurman, Howard. *Deep River and the Negro Spiritual Speaks of Life and Death.* Richmond, IN: Friends United Press, 1975.

Thurman, Howard. *Disciplines of the Spirit.* Richmond, IN: Friends United Press, 1963.

Thurman, Howard, ed. *The First Footprints – The Dawn of the Idea of the Church for the Fellowship of All Peoples: Letters Between Alfred Fisk and Howard Thurman.* San Francisco: Lawton and Alfred Kennedy, 1975.

Thurman, Howard. *Footprints of a Dream: The Story of the Church for the Fellowship of All Peoples.* New York: Harper & Row, 1959.

Thurman, Howard. *For the Inward Journey: The Writings of Howard Thurman.* Richmond, IN: Friends United Press, 1984.

Thurman, Howard. *The Greatest of These.* Mills College, CA: Eucalyptus Press, 1944.

Thurman, Howard. *The Growing Edge.* Richmond, IN: Friends United Press, 1956.

Thurman, Howard. *The Inward Journey.* New York: Harper & Row, 1961, Richmond, IN: Friends United Press, 1971.

Thurman, Howard. *Jesus and the Disinherited.* Richmond, IN: Friends United Press, 1969.

Thurman, Howard. *The Luminous Darkness.* Richmond, IN: Friends United Press, 1965.

Thurman, Howard. *Meditations for Apostles of Sensitiveness.* Mills College, CA: Eucalyptus Press, 1947.

Thurman, Howard. *Meditations of the Heart.* Richmond, IN: Friends United Press, 1953.

Thurman, Howard. *The Mood of Christmas.* Richmond, IN: Friends United Press, 1969.

Thurman, Howard. *Mysticism and the Experience of Love.* Wallingford, PA: Pendle Hill, 1961.

Thurman, Howard. *The Negro Spiritual Speaks of Life and Death.* New York: Harper & Row, 1947.

Thurman, Howard. *The Search for Common Ground: An Inquiry into the Basis of Man's Experience of Community.* Richmond, Indiana: Friends United Press, 1971.

Thurman, Howard. *Temptations of Jesus: Five Sermons.* Richmond, Indiana: Friends United Press, 1962.

Thurman, Howard, ed. *A Track to the Water's Edge: The Olive Schreiner Reader.* New York: Harper & Row, 1973.

Thurman, Howard. *With Head and Heart: The Autobigraphy of Howard Thurman.* New York: Harcourt, Brace and Jovanovich, 1979.

Tillich, Paul. *Love, Power, and Justice.* London: Oxford University Press, 1954.

Tillich, Paul. *Theology of Peace.* Louisville: Westminster/John Knox, 1990.

Townes, Emily M., ed. *A Troubling in My Soul: Womanist Perspectives on Evil and Suffering.* New York: Orbis, 1993.

Townes, Emily M., ed. *Embracing the Spirit: Womanist Perspectives on Hope, Salvation and Transformation.* New York: Orbis, 1997.

Townes, Emily M. *In a Blaze of Glory: Womanist Spirituality As Social Witness.* Abingdon, 1995.

Tutu, Desmond. *God has a Dream.* New York: Doubleday, 2004.

Tutu, Desmond. *No Future Without Forgiveness.* New York: Doubleday, 1999.

Volf, Miroslav. *Exclusion or Embrace: A Theological Exploration of Identity, Otherness, and Reconciliation.* Nashville: Abingdon, 1996.

Wallis, Jim. *The Soul of Politics: Beyond the "Religious Right" and "Secular Left."* San Diego, CA: Harcourt Brace and Company, 1994.

Washington, James Melvin, ed. *A Testament of Hope: The Essential Writings and Speeches of Martin Luther King, Jr.* New York: Harper Collins, 1986.

Washington, Raleigh and Glen Kehrein. *Breaking Down Walls: A Model for Reconciliation in an Age of Racial Strife.* Chicago: Moody Press, 1993.

Watley, William D. *Roots of Resistance.* Valley Forge, PA: Judson Press, 1985.

West, Cornel. *Democracy Matters.* New York: Penguin, 2004.

West, Cornel. *Keeping Faith: Philosophy and Race in America.* New York: Routledge, 1993.

West, Cornel. *Prophesy Deliverance! An Afro-American Revolutionary Christianity.* Philadelphia: Westminster Press, 1982.

West, Cornel. *Prophetic Fragments: Illuminations of the Crisis in American Religion and Culture.* Grand Rapids, MI: Eerdmans, 1988.

West, Cornel. *Prophetic Reflections: Notes on Race and Power in America.*

Philadelphia: Westminster Press, 1982.

West, Cornel. *Race Matters*. Boston: Beacon Press, 1991.

West, Russell W. "That His People May Be One: An Interpretive Analysis of the Pentecostal Leadership's Quest of Racial Unity." Ph.D. dissertation. Virginia Beach, VA: Regent University, 1998.

Williams, Patricia J. *The Alchemy of Race and Rights: Diary of a Law Professor.* Cambridge MA: Harvard University Press, 1991.

Wilson, William Julius. *The Bridge Over the Racial Divide: Rising Inequality and Coalition Politics.* Berkley, CA: University of California Press, 1999.

Wilson, William Julius. *The Declining Significance of Race: Blacks and Changing American Institutions.* Chicago: University of Chicago Press, 1978.

Wilson, William Julius. *Power, Racism and Privilege: Race Relations in Theoretical and Sociological Perspectives.* New York: The Free Press, 1973.

Wimberly, Anne Streaty and Edward Wimberly. *Language of Hospitality: Intercultural Relations in the Household of God.* Nashville: Cokesbury, 1989.

Wink, Walter, ed. *Peace is the Way: Writings on Nonvioence from the Fellowship of Reconciliation.* New York: Orbis Books, 2000.

Wogaman, J. Philip. *Christian Moral Judgment.* Louisville: Westminster/ John Knox Press, 1989.

Wogaman, J. Philip. *Christian Perspectives on Politics.* Philadelphia: Fortress Press, 1988.

Woodson, Carter G. *The History of the Negro Church.* Washington, DC: Associated Publishers, 1921.

Yates, Elizabeth. *Howard Thurman: Portrait of a Practical Dreamer.* New York: John Day, 1964.

Young, Josiah U. *No Difference in the Fare: Dietrich Bonhoeffer and the Problem of Racism.* Grand Rapids, MI: Eerdmans, 1998.

Zepp, Ira, Jr. The Social Vision of Martin Luther King, Jr. Carlson Publishing, 1989.

ARTICLES

Bennett, Lerone, Jr. "Eulogy of Howard Thurman: Tributes to Genius," *The African American Pulpit.* Valley Forge, PA: Judson, Winter 2001.

Carson, Clayborne, "Martin Luther King, Jr., and the African American Social Gospel," *African-American Religion: Interpretive Essays in History and Culture.* Timothy eds. Fulop and Albert Raboteau. New York: HarperPerennial, 1997.

Forester, Werner. *Theological Dictionary of the New Testament,* ed. Gerhard Kittel, translated by Geoffrey W. Bromiley. Grand Rapids: Eerdmans, 1964.

Gandhi, Mohandas K. "Nonviolence – The Greatest Force," *The World Tomorrow,* October, 1926.

Goodwin, Mary E. "Racial Roots and Religion: An Interview with Howard Thurman," *The Christian Century.* Chicago: The Christian Century, 9 May 1973.

Harding, Vincent. "We Must Keep Going: Martin Luther King, Jr. and the Future of America," *Fellowship.* New York: The Fellowship of Reconciliation, January/February, 1987.

Hunt, C. Anthony. "Beyond Toleration: Confronting the Politics of Race," *The United Methodist Connection,* Columbia, MD, January 2001. Also published by the United Methodist News Service, Nashville, TN.

Hunt, C. Anthony. "The Affirmative Action Debate Out of Focus," *The United Methodist Connection*, Baltimore, MD, 1994.

Hunt, C. Anthony. "A Black Heart from the Streets," *The Wesley Journal*, Wesley Theological Seminary, Washington, DC, February 1992.

Hunt, C. Anthony. "The Church and Reparations: More than Money," *The United Methodist Connection,* Columbia, MD, February 2002. Also published by the United Methodist News Service, Nashville, TN.

Hunt, C. Anthony. "Counting the Costs: Reflections on the Church and Just War." *The United Methodist Connection,* Columbia, MD, April 2003. Also published by the United Methodist News Service, Nashville, TN.

Hunt, C. Anthony. "Honoring Martin Luther King's Dream: A Ten Point Plan," *The West Virginia United Methodist*, Charleston, WV, February 2000, *The United Methodist Connection*, Columbia, MD, January 2001. Also published by the United Methodist News Service.

Hunt, C. Anthony. "Howard Thurman and the Identity of Jesus," *FOUNDATION THEOLOGY 2004,* Graduate Theological Foundation, South Bend, IN, 2004 (Faculty Publication Series), pp. 73-93.

Hunt, C. Anthony. "The Interpretation of the Bible in African-American Churches," in *Scripture: An Ecumenical Introduction to the Bible and Its Interpretation ,* edited by Michael J. Gorman, Peabody, MA: Hendrickson Publishing, 2005.

Hunt, C. Anthony. "The Legacy of Slavery: Church Division, Racism and the Civil War," *The African Heritage Theological Journal,* Pittsville, MD, June 2001, Vol. 7, No. 1.

Hunt, C. Anthony. "Let Us Not Forget King's Prophetic Vision," *The United Methodist Connection,* Columbia, MD, January 20, 2000.

Hunt, C. Anthony. "Martin Luther King: Resistance, Nonviolence, and Community," *Black Leaders and Ideologies in the South: Resistance and Nonviolence.* eds. Preston King and Walter Earl Fluker. London, UK: Critical Review of International Social and Political Philosophy (Taylor and Francis Ltd.), 2004.

Hunt, C. Anthony. "Multi-Cultural Leadership in the New Millennium," (*edited with John R. Schol),* The Multi-Ethnic Center for Ministry, Columbia, MD 1999.

Hunt, C. Anthony. "Redeeming the Dream: Revisiting Martin Luther King, Jr.'s Beloved Community," *The African Heritage Journal,* Pittsville, MD, June 2004, Vol. 10, No. 1.

Hunt, C. Anthony. "Time for Decisions," *The Diamondback,* University of Maryland, College Park, MD, February 1982

Hunt, C. Anthony. "UMBC Ahead of Its Time," *The Diamondback,* University of Maryland, College Park, MD, April 1982.

Hunt, C. Anthony. "When Violence Abounds: A Call to Action Against Violence," *The United Methodist Connection,* Columbia, MD, March 15, 2000.

King, Martin Luther, Jr. "Facing the Challenge of a New Age," *Fellowship.* New York: The Fellowship of Reconciliation, February, 1957.

King, Martin Luther, Jr. "My Pilgrimage to Nonviolence," *Fellowship.* New York: The Fellowship of Reconciliation, September, 1958.

King, Martin Luther, Jr. "Suffering and Faith," *The Christian Century.* Chicago, IL: The Christian Century, April 1960.

King, Martin Luther Jr. "The Unchristian Christian," *Ebony* 20. Chicago: Johnson Publishing, August 1965.

McClain, William B. "When a Dream is Deferred," *Circuit Rider,* Nashville: UM Publishing, March/April 1999.

Thurman, Howard. "Mysticism and Social Change," Eden Theological Seminary Bulletin IV. (Spring, 1939).

Thurman, Howard. "The Will to Segregate," Fellowship. New York: The Fellowship of Reconciliation, August, 1943.

Williams, Robert C. "Worship and Anti-Structure in Thurman's Vision of the Sacred," The Journal of the Interdenominational Theological Center, eds. Melva Wilson Costen and Darius Leander Swann, Atlanta, GA, Vol. XIV, Fall 1986/Spring 1987, nos. 1 & 2.

ABOUT THE AUTHOR

C. ANTHONY HUNT

A native of Washington, DC, C. Anthony Hunt is a minister in the United Methodist Church and currently serves as the Superintendent of the Baltimore Harford District in Maryland. He was previously the Executive Director of the Multi-Ethnic Center for Ministry of the United Methodist Church in Columbia, MD. Additionally, he is Professor of Practical and Systematic Theology at St. Mary's Seminary and University in Baltimore, MD, and is on the adjunct faculty at Wesley Theological Seminary in Washington, DC and the Graduate Theological Foundation in South Bend, Indiana. Dr. Hunt is a graduate of the University of Maryland, and holds advanced degrees from Troy State University, Wesley Theological Seminary and the Graduate Theological Foundation, in affiliation with Oxford University. Additionally, he has completed postdoctoral studies at St. Mary's Seminary in Baltimore, MD and the Center of Theological Inquiry at Princeton University. He is the author of *Blessed are the Peacemakers: A Theological Analysis of the Thought of Howard Thurman and Martin Luther King, Jr.* (2005), *Upon the Rock: A Model for Ministry with Black Families* (2002), and is the co-author of *Building Hope: New Church Development in the African-American Community* (1997). Additionally, he is the author of over 30 published articles and chapters on issues related to the church and society.

www.ingramcontent.com/pod-product-compliance
Lightning Source LLC
Chambersburg PA
CBHW062057270326
41931CB00013B/3114